MILDRED CONSTANTINE AND EGBERT JACOBSON

REINHOLD PUBLISHING CORPORATION, NEW YORK

# sign language

for buildings

and landscape

© 1961, Reinhold Publishing Corporation
All rights reserved
Printed in the United States of America
Library of Congress Catalog Card No. 61-13197
Designed by Elaine Lustig
Type set by Howard O. Bullard, Inc.
Printed by Comet Press
Bound by Russell Rutter Company, Inc.

# CONTENTS

The art of letters–or lettering–as distinguished from the art of literature, is rather closely related to architecture in two important ways. On the one hand, from the hieroglyphics that covered Egyptian walls to the neon signs that infest mid-twentieth century cityscapes, lettering or its equivalent has again and again had the power to break, if not to make, architecture. We have all seen in the last decade the magnificent space of the Grand Central Station's concourse eroded away by advertising–much of it pictorial as well as lettered, and all the worse for that. At the other extreme, at conferences on lettering, I have known highly critical audiences to acclaim Renaissance Revival buildings of the nineteenth century, such as Barry's Manchester Athenaeum or McKim, Mead & White's Boston Public Library, because of the extraordinary distinction of their carved inscriptions. But large areas of the world of lettering, from handwriting through book design to typewriter letter-forms, have nothing to do with buildings; and much of the large-scale lettering of signs with which this book is concerned is physically independent of architecture.

The basic relationship between architecture and lettering is of a different order, however. It is that both arts, unlike the freer arts of painting and sculpture, are bound to serve function, indeed that this is the very raison d'etre of their existence. Both are also bound in varying degree by the materials and techniques employed and to a greater degree, on the whole, than are painting or sculpture, at least in modern times.

The function of lettering is primarily to communicate and, in signs, various symbols may actually take the place of lettered words, or at least supplement them, as in the case of pointing hands, arrows, and the various established symbols of highway codes. Thus an intelligible sign, in the proper context, may be no more than a white line painted on a highway. In this way, and in the relatively simple formal elements of which letters are composed, there is a high degree of abstraction, as there is also of course in the formal elements of architecture. It is not surprising, therefore, that modern painters, from the Cubists onwards, have frequently introduced letters and even whole words into their paintings; while some of the most beautiful inscriptions of the past are found in the works of Renaissance painters such as Mantegna.

Despite the fact that a pointing hand is a representation, if a highly schematic one, of reality and other symbolic elements of conventional sign-language may owe their intelligibility to our recognition of what they represent, lettering, like architecture, is an abstract art that serves function. As with architecture, therefore, there can be awkward dichotomies between lettering that is formally beautiful, but very hard to read, and lettering that serves its prime purpose admirably–a sign reading STOP, for example–but is intrinsically ugly. But here we may allow that a major part of the function of much lettering, as expressing certain particular situations, is to be beautiful, or at least attractive; and that there is rarely justification for outright ugliness, except perhaps in the sense of the theories of the New Brutalists in architecture, which grant positive value in context to forms and textures that would be, if considered alone, rather disagreeable.

Even more than the architect today, the designer of lettering is still borne down by the weight of the past. The inherited

**PREFACE**

repertory of letter forms remains what the eclectic architects of the last two hundred years claimed that the architectural styles of the past were for them, a series of languages or dialects whose appropriate use could underline and give meaning to the expression of particular purposes. In the mid-twentieth century the use of letter forms from the past is often justified both by the continued use of inherited techniques, as in type-founding, and by the fact that it is very hard for everyone to disassociate abstract expressive value in letter forms from connotations related to the periods that first saw them perfected. Nothing could be more ridiculous than such "Gaelic" words as "bus" and "telefon" inscribed in seven-century uncials, but to the Irish who consistently use this early mediaeval lettering today for their official signs, these letter forms, like the associated Gaelic spellings, reflect patriotically their hard-won independence from England. Thus one is forced to admit that sign-language must often be an impure language, almost necessarily cosmopolitan and eclectic in many situations. Attempts to create wholly new repertories of letter forms intended for all uses, as at the Bauhaus in the 1920's, only succeeded in creating another stylism, not without intrinsic merit, but even considered as an expression of "Modernism" hardly superior to eighteenth-century Bodoni. On the other hand, the creation of a "house-style" in signs based on particular letter forms –in this case also newly invented or at least revised–by the London Underground under Frank Pick a generation ago proved to be very effective indeed. In such a situation particular forms can become rapidly and, at best, almost exclusively associated with a certain range of functions, thus acquiring the equivalent of traditional status.

There are so many different aspects to the world of lettering, and its problems have generally been studied only in the special field of book design, that the authors have wisely concentrated their attention chiefly on problems concerned with the brief and large-scale use of lettering in what are most conveniently referred to as "signs." They have to a large extent used illustrations to tell their story and to make plain by examples the very wide range of issues involved, the relative virtues and vices of various treatments, and the positive pleasure to be obtained from observing the lettering around us with sharp eyes and conscious aesthetic attention.

Henry-Russell Hitchcock

In his great book "When the Cathedrals Were White" Le Corbusier talked about his hope for the environment of the twentieth century. He felt that man must aim to produce in such an environment "those things in which reason and poetry co-exist, in which wisdom and enterprise join hands."[1]

Today's urban scene is a jungle, overgrown, malformed, a product of chaotic unplanned growth, encouraged by competition that is wasteful, unwise and immobilizing. Man struggles through a tangle of people-packed, building-choked, traffic-snarled streets—and a multitude of signs which are an assault on the senses and the eyes; all elements seem to work at cross-purposes, incomprehensible to him and contradictory to one another.

A city and its environs are far more than a fortuitous complex of streets, roads, bars, movies—each trying to attract or to compete through raucous signs. The fast-moving eye darts from pillar to post, from sky to pavement. There is neither form nor order, nor compositions and arrangements designed to slow down reactions. The country road has become a three-ring circus; the highway with its profusion and confusion of signs has become a danger trap.

Whether on Peachtree Street in Atlanta, Market Street in San Francisco, Broadway in New York, Piccadilly in London, the Piazza del Duomo in Milan, or on Main Streets throughout the world, we are confronted with a vulgar and mistaken notion of free enterprise, expressed in the sign language of our time. We are assailed with a confusion of words, names and slogans in all sizes, in all forms, in all colors and shapes—a never-ceasing roar that moves, blinks, flashes warnings, pleads and cajols, demands, reminds, but seldom instructs. In this cacaphonic bombardment, what do we look at? What do we see? Can anybody see in this impetuous, disorderly landscape of lettering?

To correct the present state of affairs by means of censorship is neither desirable nor possible. No one would wish for the colorless kind of conformity that any standardization might bring. But between standardization and the present chaotic urban environment, there is a middle ground of common interest —one which demands courage, knowledge, discipline and a sense of adventure. Discipline that involves restriction need not be censorship. At the American Institute of Architects convention in Minneapolis in August, 1955, city planner Willem Marinus Dudok said, "Restricting the liberty of use of ground, restricting the liberty of use of building, restricting the liberty of signs, all these restrictions would function for the benefit of all. The city planner must not confine himself to the ground plan only."[2]

## 1 WHAT DO THE EYES SEE?

Signs are necessary in innumerable ways. Their mission is either one of social function or of economic necessity. Those signs that inform and instruct must be disentangled from those that offer goods and services. The general arrangement of both public and private signs should have a character and expression that is congenial to and beneficial for the individual and the community. To treat the look and the language of our signs as something apart from the problems of our urban and rural scene is a sad and oft-repeated mistake. Signs are the responsibility of a team—the architect, designer, planner and local authority. Together they can compose, sort out and plan the ways of enhancing the look of the modern city.

Properly understood, placed and designed, all of our signs can become a new kind of heraldry, enriching the structures and the landscape. Our failure is due to immaturity and irre-

9

sponsibility in recognizing this aspect of the vital city of today. When we recognize what is worth preserving in our customs and surroundings, and abandon our anachronistic contradictions, we can create a pattern that will endure and be beautiful.

The purpose of this book is to relate the signs of our times to twentieth century culture and planning; to emphasize the relationship of lettering to a single building, to mass, and to open spaces. We shall applaud and illustrate the positive achievements of artists, architects, designers and planners in the following pages. We hope to stimulate awareness among those responsible by discussing the complex nature of the problem and the possibilities for solution; to emphasize the basic element of esthetics in the art of lettering, and show how it may be maintained without sacrificing variety or practical and economic needs; to encourage efforts on the part of artists and designers to further develop the art of lettering.

The editors of the "Architectural Review" have shown us in their articles "Outrage" and "Counter-attack" that the "fate of British landscape is in balance" and their outspoken and uncompromising articles have served as a constant pointing finger to the lessons we must understand and apply.[3]

The authors of this book wish to thank the late Alvin Lustig for his ideas, for his vigilance, and for his talents, which have all contributed to bringing this book into being. Without Philip Johnson, the Yale Graduate School of Design's seminar "Signs for Streets and Buildings" in 1954, and the Museum of Modern Art's exhibition "Signs in the Street," also in 1954, this book could not have been prepared. Special thanks are due to Herbert Bayer, Marcel Breuer, Arthur Drexler, Ralph Eckerstrom, Victor Gruen, Jose Luis Sert, Lewis Mumford, Henry-Russell Hitchcock for their helpful ideas, encouragement and statements. To Elaine Lustig our thanks and profound admiration for the lucid design of this volume.

Mildred Constantine and Egbert Jacobson

Goldberg Clothing Store, New York City, 1937.

Untitled drawing. Saul Steinberg. "The New Yorker Magazine, Inc.," 1949.

(Above) Road sign, Springfield, Massachusetts.
(Below) Highway U.S. 1, Maryland. Clog-up caused by tight lanes, poles and signs, crowding, inadequate shoulders.

Sicilian street scene.

Cupola of St. Peters, and Esso sign, Rome.

(Above; below right) Signs on Broadway, New York City.

(Below left) Los Angeles street scene.

Sign on Broadway, New York City.

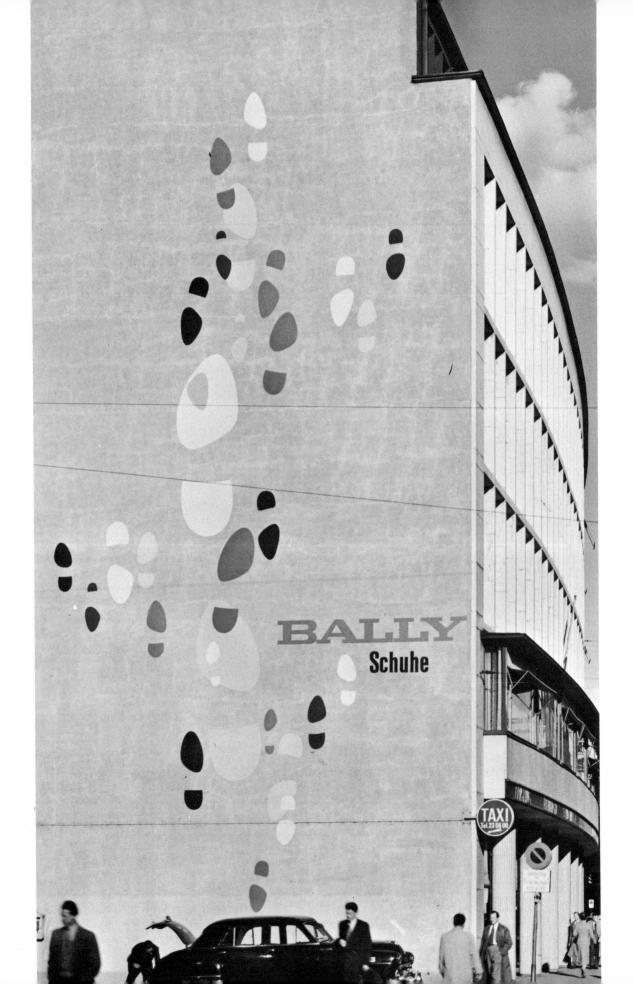

nted wall advertisement, Bally Shoes, Zurich,
itzerland, 1956. J. Müller-Brockmann, Designer.
proximately 75 feet high. Note taxi sign.

A city is made and designed. Its essence is determined by the demands of its time. Our twentieth century cities have become ugly because of the disintegration of man's satisfactions. But the question remains, "If visual satisfactions are important to good living everywhere, how much more vital (are they) in big cities where the whole scene is man-made?"[4] Visual satisfactions do not come from the necessary ingredients of sanitation, perfect sewerage and fashion; nor from the incongruities of decoration, signs and symbols.

The charm of the great cities of the world lies in the orchestration of their streets and plazas, in the preservation of their great squares, their old buildings and monuments and landmarks—all those elements which characterize a civilization. Every single component contributes to the total scene. These cities reflect the changes wrought slowly through the centuries.

The art of building cities is an ancient one and cities everywhere functioned as focal points in the diffusion of culture. In Medieval times, as well as during the days of the Roman Republic, men trained in the philosophy and skills of city planning and construction were employed by the rulers of cities as a matter of course. They belonged to a small cultivated aristocracy whose interest lay not only in statecraft but in the arts and sciences of the day. Rome, Paris, London are remarkable for their large open spaces, the layout of their squares. The buildings masses and the breathing spaces were all welded together with concern for the intimate, the spectacular and the colorful. In the great squares of the world and off their corners, there is scarcely a street which does not present a handsome sight to the viewer, scarcely a turn that does not offer a surprise.

The link between the twentieth century city and its past has been broken by the machine age which produced the chaotic expansion of the modern city, its unwieldy transportation systems and agglomeration of signs—all of which we are asked to accept as characteristic of a moral and economic democracy. Walter Schwagenscheidt in his book "Ein Mensch Wandert Durch die Stadt" states plaintively but pointedly that "man should not accept such treatment from a machine."[5] It is not a question of acceptance; it is a demanding challenge to harmonize the practical phases of traffic and the ever-changing demands of communication, to blend the economic and social needs with the intangible, spiritual expressions that make a city the symbol of its time.

Are our cities faithful reflections of the life of our time? The absence of planning which has placed the wrong things in the wrong places is particularly demonstrated by the information and communication signs—the overwhelming urban embellishments of the twentieth century. These signs go beyond a manifestation of the desire to advertise. Throughout the world an indifference has permitted such blights as the Esso sign seen in juxtaposition to a basilica in Rome (see page 15). This cannot be excused as a gesture of spontaneity. It is not a convenience of communication, nor an adornment in the cityscape. Does it lend vitality to its environment? The vulgar stocking-covered leg above the low building on a Los Angeles street is lacking in charm. It is startling, but is it effective? Broadway's well-known signs do not all blink, do not all have the vulgarity of twenty-five foot capital letters, but they present Broadway with little inspiration and a great concentration of ugliness (see pages 16-17).

What is Broadway supposed to be? We think of New York, and Broadway and Times Square come to mind; Piccadilly symbolizes London, just as St. Peters and the Place de la Concord

## 2 CITYSCAPE

symbolize Rome and Paris. Do Broadway and Piccadilly really represent New York and London? Are they anachronisms or are they still valid in terms of the 1960's, of the 1980's? Are they uniquely suited to their purposes? Is the plan, the architecture, the furniture and the decoration of Broadway and Piccadilly suited to the total concepts and needs of these modern public outdoor arenas? Do the signs on Broadway serve their function to identify, to inform, to decorate? Are they in keeping with our concepts of modern communication, with modern display techniques? WOULD YOU CHANGE BROADWAY???

"There are no ordinary days on Broadway," says Jose Luis Sert. "It is a perpetual parade which produces a festive atmosphere . . . like a big stage."[6] As he wrote in "Architectural Forum," "This festivity requires changing disguises. Broadway should always be a container for changing architecture. It should be nothing more than a facade, a clothes hanger on which to hang a sign, spectacular displays and advertisements. Broadway should be an enormous open space with its space units capable of definition and re-definition. The signs on Broadway should not be on the surface. They should move in depth. People are below . . . activity of life is above . . . For too long the advertising people have been engaging not the great artists but fourth-rate imitators of the great artists. Why not get the real thing in advertising art and display? . . . Our symbols are stale today. Instead of flat billboards, elements should be used in depth."[7]

When Sert gave the students of the Harvard Graduate School of Design a project to improve Times Square, he did not ask for an abstract reverie. "Times Square is a noisy area," he told his students and directed them to try to keep it that way. "No trees," said Sert. "Trees are not right for a central entertainment area. Plan to circulate cars and people; for open plaza areas; create new palettes for the advertising signs." The project produced some encouraging ideas: new structures were created to carry advertisements; blank walls were constructed to hide garages; the original character of old buildings was restored by stripping them of defacing signs (see pages 28-29).

Lewis Mumford, long a champion of civic sanity, states, "Those shabby and flashy facts of life which constitute the signs on Broadway have a kind of rhythm which makes Broadway nothing more than a carnival. What might have the effect of lightness and relaxation at night becomes mean and rather tawdry in daylight. Don't take away the color and the brilliance. See if the rhythm and lights produced by traffic can be brought into more cohesion with the conscious play of lights produced by the street signs. Since this carnival spirit is in a sense spoiled by traffic, perhaps its meaning can be restored by the removal of traffic. Broadway is also a commercial street and these elements have grown to be dominant. But the agglomeration of signs is an indication of a state of mind. The signs grow chaotic and their total lack of organization results in a nullification of their prime purpose–communication."[8]

According to the "Architectural Review," "The symbolic importance of Times Square to the American nowadays is derived more from night advertising than from the frivolity offered. With darkness, that particular brand of nondescript architecture disappears and the signs become the architecture of night. That disturbing lack of relationship between the sign and the building that supports it is eliminated."[9]

Le Corbusier calls New York "an unfinished city . . . a vast nocturnal festival . . . a limitless cluster of jewels . . . a fairy catastrophe. "What disorder, what impetuosity, its furniture all unkempt."[10] Yet this fairy tale of myriad lights turns to a nightmare in the daylight!

If it costs a half million and has 10,000 bulbs, it's wonderful! So one might characterize the signs on Broadway. In 1956, Walter Winchell reported that the real big show on Broadway was the outdoor spectacular electrics: a Bond waterfall (since removed); a mammoth Pepsi-Cola bottle (since removed); bubbles frothing on a soap ad; a smoker blowing rings; signs for chewing gum, sparkling water and a movie—each a city-block long. The Disney technique of animation was transferred to lights.[11] How much did this provide in the way of fitness and delight? There is an undisputed advertising value in beauty—these vulgarities and irresponsibilities do not perform a service to the advertiser. Nor do the harassed open spaces and false monumentalities which give us little satisfaction.

The "Architectural Review" calls Piccadilly Circus in London "a glittering network of neon signs," and declares, "How little the secret of their vulgar but vigorous appeal is generally understood can be judged from the pathetic design which has been suggested to replace them. The planners are trying to give some coherence and at the same time improve the traffic flow . . . they propose to open up the existing intimate circle into a large bleak square. Since all of the architecture dissolves in the blaze of lights and becomes merely a scaffolding for the signs, the buildings will not be missed; the signs will . . . The new design is an insipid jigsaw of small designs straitjacketed into a rectangular panel . . . it can hardly provide the same gay, unfettered riot of signs it replaces."[12] (See pages 30-31.)

The "Architectural Review" knows that Piccadilly Circus cannot remain a fairy tale which appears only in the black night and disappears magically in the morning. It continues, "In Piccadilly Circus architecture and advertising must be indivisible." This is the crux of the problem. These associative symbols on Piccadilly exist only for night life as part of an exciting scene. Inevitably, through natural and forced obsolescence the Broadways and Piccadillys of the world must undergo a change. Philip Johnson has pointed out that it is not the architect's job to create spontaneity, but rather to create the background for spontaneity. However, this cannot come about through the efforts of the architect alone. The vigilance of the lawmakers, the city planners, the architects and the artists of advertising and display are necessary to bring this about. An ordered design need not be, as the "Architectural Review" calls the Piccadilly plan, "rationed form"—controlled, coordinated, emasculated. If the advertising design is to be integral with the architecture of the street, it must be able to withstand the exposure of daylight as well as the darkness of night.

The "Review" presents some ideas for the new Piccadilly plan which are similar in many respects to the Harvard students' suggestions. It urges that the signs must not be an afterthought and should be taken much further, that the advertising should become indivisible from the architecture. Some of the suggestions follow:

1) Using the whole building as a signboard without interfering with or relating to interior space.

2) Providing blank end walls at angles to the main plaza and using them for giant signs.

3) Continuation of the structural frame of a building which contains the service parts provides a perfect armature for the sign and is as pleasant to look at in the daytime as it is at

night. All electric wiring can be housed within the building.
4) Using the flat roof for free-shaped designs.
5) Sky signs to span the streets and provide an artificial sky.
6) Free-standing framework towers to make architecture and advertising indivisible.
7) A concrete post jungle gym; pre-cast panels which are removable, large scale, similar but not identical in texture, structure, shape and finish.

All of our past errors might be eliminated and our hopes for the future realized in the opportunities available to us throughout the world today. One answer is of course not applicable to all our problems. Old cities with many centers, and new cities, both large and small, present very different conditions. Lincoln Center, for example, is one of many centers in an old city of which Broadway and Times Square have become a stereotype.

Brasilia, on the other hand, is an entirely new city. What considerations are given to the necessity for signs in a new city? After a recent visit there, George Nelson said, "Brasilia has the aspect of an urban phenomenon, but not that of a city. There are two reasons for this look of a city-not-yet-a-city. Lucio Costa, the planner, gives the first and more important reason: Brasilia, he says, is a framework, not a city, because a city cannot be built in three years. What impressed me more than Costa's sensible explanation was the evident fact that Brasilia was planned to meet the conditions of modern existence, paramount of which are the conditions created by the automobile and by public surface transportation systems. Thus, the main avenue of Brasilia, while a noble thoroughfare, is not an avenue in any recognizable traditional sense. The avenue, as delineated by Haussmann, is a thoroughfare lined by coordinated facades. The main avenue of Brasilia looks like a piece out of a super-highway, flanked by parks, in which glass and marble towers arise in a rather irregular fashion."[13]

Nelson continues, "The visual apparatus of a city—all the street furniture—signs, benches, bus stations, lighting standards, and so on will not count for very much. In the more congested parts of the city, still wide open by conventional urban standards, they will still count, but not for very much. Brasilia, I think, poses an entirely new problem: the coordinated design of private and public signs and street furniture generally, so crucial a means for reducing the visual chaos in ordinary urban centers, is important, but no longer crucial. Brasilia as it stands is a park with buildings in it; most cities are buildings with occasional parks among them. In the typical traditional city, signs and all the urban accessories which present themselves to the passerby can be used to alleviate the monotony of streets, to enliven drab facades, or functionally, to enable the driver to find his way through the tangle of traffic. In Brasilia, where planning is the dominant thought, it is hard to imagine these devices being inserted as afterthoughts. However, whether planned in a coordinated way or not, their relative importance will be less than it has ever been in a city of comparable size and importance."

But Brasilia is only one of two entirely new cities to come into being in our time; the other is Chandigarh. The lessons which they can teach may become apparent only after many, many years. What of the old city which must change to keep pace with the demands of changing society? What do the planners think? What do the architects envision? They are sufficiently resourceful to round out their concepts with results. Around the world there are signs in the cityscape that point the way.

Place Vendome, Paris.

Piazza San Marco, Venice.

(Above) Place de la Concorde, Paris.

(Below) Panorama of Vatican City as seen from the cupola of St. Peter's, Rome.

(Facing page) Tivoli Gardens, Copenhagen, Denmark. Traditional symbols of merchandise offered within stores.

(Above) Old house on the Battery, New York City.

(Center) Fabrikant Bros., Canal Street, New York City.

(Below) CBS Television Studio, looking north on Broadway from Fifty-second Street, New York City.

"Times Square Tomorrow," a project of Harvard University's Graduate School of Architecture, 1955; under the direction of Jose Luis Sert, Dean. Costantino Nivola, sculptor and instructor of design fundamentals, developed technique of model-making. Note towers and structures for advertising. Drawing shows revolving cubes of various colors suggested for display and advertising messages. Blank walls on added parking garages reserved for applied advertising.

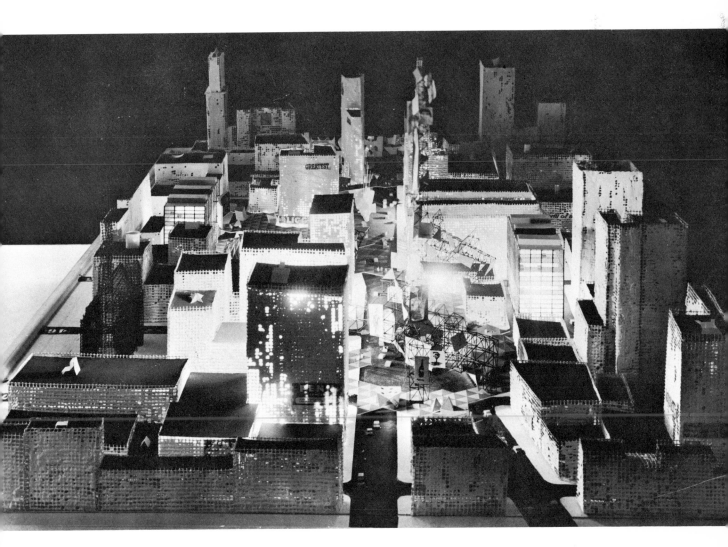

(Below) Night view, Piccadilly Circus, north side.

(Facing page) Model of building proposed to replace existing structures. Cotton, Ballard and Blow, Architects, 1959.

"The Paris Bit." Oil. Stuart Davis, 1959. Collection:
Whitney Museum of American Art, New York. An
artist composes the elements of the city.

Day and night views, Breuninger department store, Stuttgart, Germany. Gottfried Prölss, Designer. At night architecture disappears.

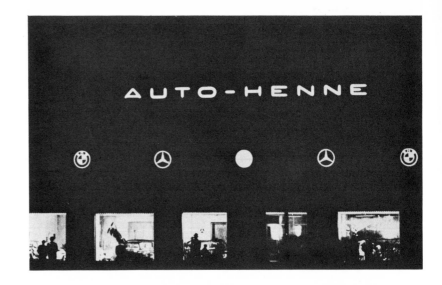

(Above) Auto showroom, Henne, Munich. The trademarks of the factories represented make effective and decorative identification. The firm name is executed in fluorescent tubing.

(Center) An illuminated advertisement for Frères Philips on an interior glass wall of the railway station in Hamburg. The name in outline letters retains a pleasing relationship to the other elements in the composition.

(Below) Het Parool, lees die krant, Leidse Plein, Amsterdam. Lighted lines and arrows decorate old building of daily newspaper.

(Facing page) Night view of London. Underground subway symbol in foreground.

(Above) An old building in Cologne carries illuminated advertising. Here again architecture disappears, and the diversity of advertising is given unity by restraint and simplicity.

(Below) Night advertising, Zurich, Switzerland, as seen from moving auto.

(Above) Monogram on facade and figures on side wall are ceramic on brick. Tokyo. A tapestry use of wall. (See page 115.)

(Below) Painted symbol for Southern Countries Gas Company, Atlanta, Georgia.

(Right) Byrrh, Vin Tonique, a painted wall in Paris.

(Below left) Bavarian Mortgage and Loan Bank, Munich. Painted in a light greenish-blue on to the rough plaster, the symmetrical design gives form to the large area.

(Below right) Lincoln's Inn, Heraldic Office. Letters applied on two facades. The wall surface, uncluttered, gives quiet vitality to the city scene.

(Top) "Around the World in 80 Days," painted wall on Fifty-second Street and Broadway, New York City, 1956.

(Below) Parade Square, Zurich, Switzerland, 1948. Road signs and street markings typical of Swiss street system.

Metropolitain, entrance gate to Paris subway. Structure and lettering designed by Hector Guimard, c. 1900.

Bally Shoes, Zurich, Switzerland, 1956. J. Müller-Brockmann, Designer. A gaily painted wall in the city. (See page 18.)

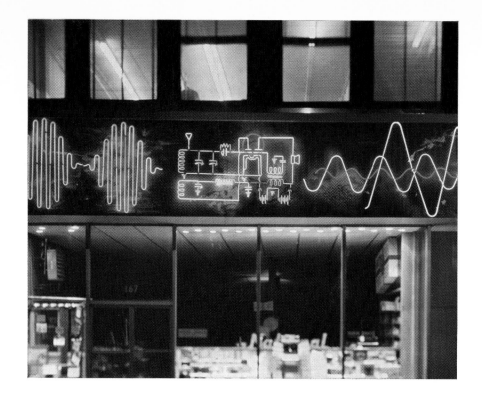

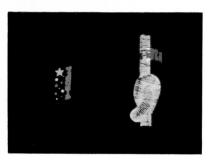

(Above) Radio Shack Corp. store, Boston, Mass., 1950. Carl Koch & Associates, Architects; Gyorgy Kepes, Consultant. A painted porcelain enamel panel is the background for electric light tubes creating an abstract linear pattern.

(Below) Night scenes, Tokyo, Japan, 1958.

(Top) Olivetti Sales Corp., Chicago, Illinois, 1957. Barancik & Conte, Architects. The Olivetti name and numerals are plexiglas; the name is in white and is back-lighted, the numerals are multicolored and flash on and off at random.

(Bottom) Columbia Broadcasting System, Color Studio 72, New York City, 1951. William Golden, Designer. The CBS symbol contains a color kaleidoscope. Numerals always appear in the same letter form—the family identity is retained. (See page 162.)

Tokyo at night, 1958. Signs for restaurants, sa
vitamins, medicines. Abstract symbols, employir
constant or changing lights are in use througho
the world.

Philadelphia Saving Fund Society, Philadelphia, 1932. Roof sign designed by Howe & Lescaze, Architects. View from Logan Square, and detail of sign; letter form adapted from Gothic Condensed.

Store sign, San Francisco.

46

Almost a complete anthology of letters and numbers can be found on buildings seen throughout the world today.

Under ideal conditions, a building is identified by its architectural character rather than by a sign. Public buildings, such as the Eiffel Tower, St. Peter's, Westminster Abbey, and even recent buildings, such as the United Nations Secretariat, the Guggenheim Museum, the Seagram Building, give evidence of this.

Perhaps, however, one cannot expect factories, apartment houses, office or university buildings, railroad stations, or trucks and trains to be so readily identifiable. In these instances, name and number are necessary for the pedestrian, the postman and the motorist.

Thus, the architect and designer is given the opportunity to introduce lettering as an architectural detail enriching the facade of the building. An inscription that informs can enliven the whole and become an element of decoration. Character and legibility are the first essential requirements of a statement of identification. Materials, structure, style, size and placement can all contribute to the visual effect.

The placement of an inscription on a building should of course make identification simple, direct and immediate. The message, however, must reach viewers under different conditions involving different distances. Old buildings, new buildings; buildings on open squares or in narrow long streets; isolated buildings and row buildings; buildings in the suburban and rural scenes—all present individual problems.

In the buildings of the past, exterior wall surfaces were mainly stone, granite and marble. Inscriptions were conventional only in the method of application. However, the placement on a facade, a door, a gate, was greatly varied, and the beauty and diversity of letter forms abounded.

During the last hundred years, however, our environment has been dramatically transformed; our architecture has evolved to meet the demands of industrialization—demands which have included new building types—from railroad stations to skyscrapers. In the last thirty years our buildings have been sheathed in steel, glass and aluminum. Letters cannot be incised directly on such exterior skins and other methods of sign application have come into use. In our time, elegance and proportion of letters have been further enhanced by the variety of material employed, complementing or contrasting with the surface material of the building. Advances in illumination provide new promise for the daytime and nighttime scenes.

Identification of a building is expressed in many ways. The name of a building can be spelled out and treated as a frieze (see page 57); where brevity is desired, initials can be used as a vignette (see page 53). The number, a necessity of urban environment, sometimes with a symbol, is often employed as the sole means of identification (see Chapter 6).

## 3 NAME AND NUMBER

When the identification sign becomes an independent element, as on a pylon or a standard, greater freedom is possible for the designer (see Chapter 5) but character, legibility and fitness are still the basic ingredients. Dramatic effect may be heightened through stylization, color, and of course, lighting.

Identification combined with modern advertising display methods can produce handsome effects without abusing the facade of a building or the integrity of the architectural concept.

Name and number on a building or store front can make a visual contribution—whether treated as a single elaborate element or an independent structural element—if the function is straightforwardly expressed and combined with aesthetic considerations for the total scene.

(Facing page)
(Above left) Tug Boat Tracy, East River, New York.

(Above center) Building, Hong Kong. Flag in white and red used in place of permanent sign.

(Above right) Store, Hong Kong. The sign is three stories high; metal letters are used on a slate panel.

(Below) Bauhaus, Dessau, Germany, 1925-26; Walter Gropius, Architect; Herbert Bayer, Designer. Downward emphasis on rounded A helps letter form to adjust to vertical placement.

Citroen, illumination of the Eiffel Tower—despoiled by badly conceived advertising.

(Right) prm shop, Florence, Italy, 1956. White letters painted on glass, pencil line frame rounded at corners are handsomely suited to arched windows; condensed lower case letters appropriate to space.

(Center left) American Airlines, New York City.

(Below left) Fly TWA, Paris. The italic form is an effective use of the sans letter because of change in size of letters and relationship to background frame. Fly TWA is good advertisement and identification.

(Below right) Towson Plaza, Towson, Maryland, 1959. Brownjohn, Chermayeff & Geismar, Designers. The letter T is 10 feet high on the north wall. Scale of T to square label carrying full name is excellent.

Mid-Wilshire Medical Building, Los Angeles, 1951. Victor Gruen, Architect. Restrained use of initial letters on side wall; note Mid-Wilshire Pharmacy sign, garage and street markings. Letter form adapted from Futura Bold. All signs shown here and on facing page indicate expressions possible with sans-serif letters.

(Above) Cafe sign, bronze, c. 1900; designer unknown. Collection of Joseph H. Heil, New York.

(Below) Hagemeyer's City Magazijn, shop front in Utrecht, Holland, designed c. 1900.

(Facing page) Addo-X Corporation, New York City, 1957. Symbol designed by Hans Lindblom and Oscar Nitschke of Batir Design Associates, Architects. Screen projects beyond glass facade to house sign. Letters appear three-dimensional by being placed to face in two directions at opposite ends of clear plastic cylinders.

(Left) German Electrical Industries Exhibit, Barcelona International Exposition, 1929. Mies van der Rohe, Architect; Gerhardt Severain, Designer. Sansserif adaptation.

(Below left) Abby Aldrich Rockefeller Sculpture Garden, Museum of Modern Art, New York City, 1955. Philip Johnson, Architect. Letter form thought to be a variation of Clarendon extended, a rounded, sculptured letter in bronze on grey brick wall.

(Below right) Harper & Reynolds, Los Angeles. Size of letters and placement on facade make effective composition. All three signs on this page are used as decorative bands on the walls.

(Top left) Brulerie Oriental, shop at Sète in southern France. Sans-serif capitals with generous spacing contrast with lacy grille background.

(Top right) Orient Line, London. Incised, painted letters, gently italicized, decorate wood fascia.

(Below left) Beverly-Landau apartment building, Beverly Hills, California.

(Below right) The Chase Manhattan Bank, New York City, 1960. Skidmore, Owings & Merrill, Architects; Brownjohn & Geismar, Designers. Precise and mechanical letterforms, tightly spaced on black band, dramatize the entrance.

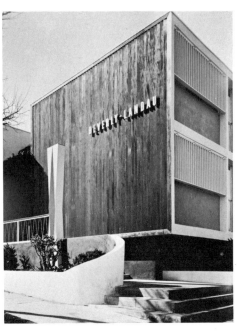

Cineac, adjacent to de Bijenkorf department store, Rotterdam, Holland, 1953. Marcel Breuer and A. Elzas, Architects; Daniel Schwarzman, Consultant. Scale of letters against dark red brick is very effective. Wires holding neon letters reflect in glass, making lively pattern. Repetition of name in neon tubes on aluminum plaque in condensed form is an expressive device. (See pages 202-3.)

De Bijenkorf department store, Rotterdam, Holland,
1953. Marcel Breuer and A. Elzas, Architects; Daniel
Schwarzman, Consultant. Day and night views of
sign. Grain and color of teak, width and weight of
letters, placement on facade all contribute to excel-
lence. Lighting from behind creates a halo around
letters. (See pages 202-3.)

(Above) Olivetti retail store, Torino, Italy. Gianan-tonio Bernasconi, Architect. The familiar squared-off, lower case sans-serif letters designed by Giovanni Pintori are painted on the window. The neon tube letters retain the original form.

(Below) Olivetti retail store, Savona, Italy.

(Top) Container Corporation of America, Greens-
boro Plant, South Carolina. (Below) Plant in Los
Angeles, California; Egbert Jacobson, Designer. The
symbol is no longer in use.

(Top) Wall of plant in Brewton, Alabama, Herbert Bayer, Designer; (Below left) Valley Forge Plant, Pennsylvania; (Below right) Company truck. The family identity is retained in spite of variety of applications and materials. A local plant sometimes is identified along with the parent company and sometimes forcefully stated on a spur wall.

(Above left) Stabilimento Grafico Cartotecnico, an office supply shop, Milan, Italy. A single identifying line on the lower edge of a diffused light panel.

(Above right) Plume of Feathers Hotel, England. Right facade carries a sans-serif letter with an awkward relationship of large initial letter to balance of word; spacing is tight and unrelated to windows. The sweep, and decorative quality of the applied letters on the left facade make a contrast to painted wall.

(Below left) British Ropes, 18 South Street, New York City. This old shop front near the Fulton Fish Market has a quiet sure elegance. The white letters on the white framed fascia, the striped awnings and the monogram in the oval label are effective.

(Below right) Apothecary shop, Parade Square, Zurich. Contrast the old building and fascia letters with the advertising on streetcars. This is typical of European restraint.

(Top left) Fruit Industries, Ltd., Chicago. Stenciled letters on old brick. Scale is well suited to low building wall and wide street.

(Top right) Insignia on freight cars of Chicago, Northwestern Railroad. An example of distinguished lettering.

(Below) Trucks for Société Geigy, Basle, Switzerland. Lanfranco Bombelli Tiravanti, Architect; Gerard Ifert, Designer. Signs on planes, trains and trucks are part of our landscape.

Herman Miller Furniture Company, Los Angeles. On glass or on brick, letters and numbers retain their decorative character.

(Top) 404—Numerals on a brick house in Chicago. Condensed form and double outline give extra emphasis against brick pattern. Connected numerals have a continuity that creates a plaque-like element.

(Below left) Woodley Medical Building, Los Angeles, 1956. Victor Gruen, Architect. Applied letters and numerals contrast with rustic background materials.

(Below right) W 404, Coast Guard ship in Sturgeon Bay, Wisconsin.

(Right) Turntable Cafe, Festival of Britain, 1951. Gordon Cullen, Designer. Wall and sign is given particular emphasis and interest by elegant Egyptian letters and area of painted brick.

(Below left) Regatta Restaurant, Festival of Britain, 1951. Mischa Black, Designer. Gold letters and symbol hold their own against busy grain on wall.

(Below right) Bar sign in Transportation Center, Philadelphia, 1957. Vincent G. Kling, Architect. Bravura of letters seem sufficient and more acceptable than the stylized caricature of pointing finger. Compare this pointing with the arrow on the cafe wall.

(Above) Sea and Ships Pavilion, South Bank Exhibition, London, 1951. Movement and shadows contribute to interest; patterned wood seems a little rustic against marble wall. Figure to the right seems overscaled and crude.

(Below) Bar, Restaurant, Transportation Center, Philadelphia, 1957. Vincent G. Kling, Architect. Stylized arrows and color provide a light note on conventional brick background.

General Motors Technical Center, Detroit, 1954.
Eero Saarinen & Associates, Architects; Alvin and
Elaine Lustig, Designers. Bright anodized aluminum
letters are carried on a gray aluminum background.

Mondawmin Shopping Center, Baltimore, Maryland.
Fisher, Nes, Campbell & Associates, Architects;
Elaine Lustig, Designer. Name in one and three lines,
and Mondawmin symbol used on building, tower,
letterheads. (See page 126.)

(Facing page) Volksschule, Stuttgart, Germany. Gottfried Prölss, Designer; executed by E. Schindler. The bold simplicity of the letters contrasts with the playful movement of the stanchion.

Geological Museum, London. One of a series of well-designed signs executed by the Maintenance Division of the Ministry of Works. Lettering in gold on a dark blue ground.

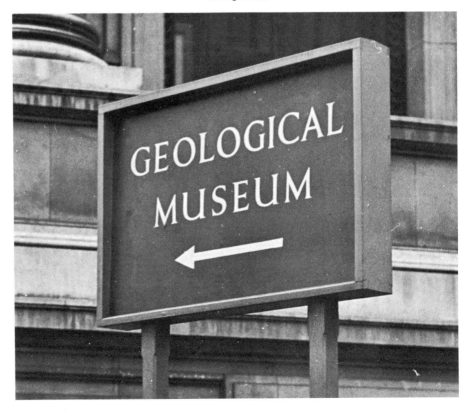

The first Greek epigraphs, those poetical inscriptions placed upon tombs, columns, sculptures and public monuments, influenced the lettering used by the Renaissance sculptors and painters. Statues by Donatello and Ghiberti bore inscriptions, and artists such as Montegna introduced into painting the simulated epigraph (see page 79).

The ancient Greek monuments presented to the Renaissance artists a more or less single, unvaried style. Throughout the course of Roman history there evolved considerable differences. These variations expressed differences of function as well as of technique. They also expressed a more subjective attitude toward beauty, legibility and decoration. Thus, many letters of individuality were produced by the great Renaissance artists. While these letters were regular, possessing great refinement and stability, the letters in humanist manuscripts were freehand, so to speak, with remarkable individuality and style.

In the union of disciplines of epigraphy and paleography and humanistic script we have the origins of the design of type for the first printed books. Movable type, invented in Europe in the fifteenth century, came late to western civilization. The twentieth century use of our inherited letter forms and their application to contemporary building has been dominated by printing.

Judging from the letters seen on buildings and signs today, there is evidently little agreement on what constitutes the well-designed letter form. It must be assumed that architects and designers make every effort to use what they consider interesting and appropriate letters, but often the letters used are far from legible or beautiful in the opinion of many scholars in the field. It is therefore fair to ask the question, "Are some designs superior to others and on what grounds?"

Sorting out the characteristics of a good letter is an interesting puzzle. The viewer's previous experience and conditioned reflexes play an important part in his subjective appraisal. A man familiar with the best Greek and Roman letters will have a point of view different from one who is not. It frequently happens that the devotee of the classics is unfamiliar with modern forms and is even opposed to them for reasons difficult to explain except in terms of sentiment.

Assuming that it is possible to be completely objective about letter forms, what standards are demanded by the viewer whose taste is cultivated and knowledgeable? What is his rationale for separating the good letter from the bad? What does he consider faults or limitations of form or style?

## 4 LETTERING

What does he know about classic letters? He will say that they are mainly characterized by beauty of form: freely drawn curves, elegant proportions of width, height, and thickness of line and serif. But he will also know that not all classic lettering is good. Awkward relationships in all these details are common in many of the inscriptions of the best periods; certain letters reveal themselves as noticeably superior to others. In other words, a perfect alphabet probably could not be found in any one inscription, but would have to be carefully chosen from several.

But even if such an alphabet were composed, no one would propose that it be accepted as a model for any inscription on any structure. Its very classicism brings with it a character suitable only to certain buildings and very few signs.

The Greeks and Romans regarded the letter as a work of art, and classical lettering reflects this strongly felt attitude. But the rationale—the classic ideal beauty of form and proportion—is difficult to use as a standard today. In the twentieth century, beauty is not the single determining criterion. There are at least two others—legibility and style appropriate to the nature and application of the message. The application is indeed more complicated than just the wording; it involves placement and detailing, and the need for distinction or instant recognition.

Many modern designers have thought to modify the classic letters by adding some personal preference of proportion or curve, or perhaps by translating the incised forms into metal or other material. Unless such changes are made by experts, the results are likely to be unfortunate. Modifying the serifs (which have their origins either in the technique of chiseling, or in the geometric precision of a compass and ruling pen) or eliminating them affects appearances so completely that changes in all proportions are usually required.

Let us examine one first-rate design based on an ideal Roman letter to see how modification affects its character and legibility. The Futura alphabet was designed by the German Paul Renner in 1927 for the Bauer Type Foundry (see page 96). There is an evenness of structure and over-all uniformity of stroke which is handsome without being overly assertive. The design lends itself most readily to the frieze treatment so common in modern architecture, particularly because, like the Roman letter, it can be condensed or extended without loss of character or linear legibility. For example, Severain used the Futura in a most extended form for the Mies building, shown on page 57. There are those who disagree as to the general success of Renner's Futura. Some question the small arc of the D as compared with the full circle of the O. Others dislike the narrow E and F and the short cross-stroke of the t and f. However, there is general agreement about the elegance and forthrightness of Futura.

There are a great many very handsome alphabets created by designers whose judgment of form and proportion is the result of long and devoted study. Thus, styles appropriate to every use and material are at the disposal of the architect or sign-maker who has to choose the alphabet that best suits the character of his statement.

Calligraphy also inherited the characteristics of the freely painted and drawn letter, and the letters and initials used in miniatures and illuminations. The modification of a letter into the italic form derived from the cursive style. Among the earliest are the Latin scripts, followed by Elizabethan handwriting, and the cursive style of Art Nouveau hand-lettering of which Civilité, a French type, is still in use (see page 102). Today script type fonts exist of many expressions. Cast in metal, the cursive style can present many attitudes—whimsy, flourish, movement. Some of the letters are imitative of brush script; others are light and airy, characteristic of certain pen forms; some are looped with mechanical regularity; others appear more freely drawn. However free these styles appear, casting in metal requires studied precision of such elements as verticality, movement, stress, shading and spacing. Their application to architecture has rarely been notable. Too often the use of a script style, especially as a signature, is illogical, inconsistent with the material employed, and out of context with its background. The success of the calligraphic letter depends on its most personal expression: it can be clear or garbled, soft or hard. Authority comes from the designer. (See page 55.)

The long tradition of modification and personal expression of letter forms is known to us today because letters were integral parts of works of art that bear the signatures of the artists who created them.

"I Saw the Figure Five in Gold." Oil on composition board. Charles Demuth, 1949. Courtesy of the Metropolitan Museum of Art, The Alfred Stieglitz Collection.

In the early Renaissance many treatises appeared describing, recording, and commenting on the design of the Roman alphabet. They bear witness to the seriousness of the concern of Quattrocento artists and humanists with the creation of a new script based on the Roman example. Millard Meiss, the noted art historian, writes of Dürer, "Just as in his speculation about the human figure Dürer had come to recognize more than one beautiful form and one canon of proportion, so in his account of Roman capitals in the "Underweysung der Messung" (1525) he presented more than one perfect example of each letter. He offered for each letter the ratio 1:9 as well as 1:10, and two or more shapes, recommending to the reader the use of one 'weliche dir am besten gefuhlt' (with which he felt best). Thus Dürer . . . undermined the central concept of the earlier theorists–that of a single perfect form. Without abandoning geometry and numerical law they opened the door to multiformity and to individual taste."[14]

The architecture of the twentieth century, set mainly in the cityscape of past centuries, bears inscriptions incorporating new ideas and new information. Considerations of new media, economy, durability, and rivalry are to be reckoned with. Thus the challenge to the artists and designers of letter forms is to benefit from history while searching for new means of expression. The grammar and vocabulary of twentieth century architecture came into being with new technology and new materials. The designers of twentieth century architectural letters must also search for appropriate new forms and symbols and at the same time retain their uncompromising personal touch.

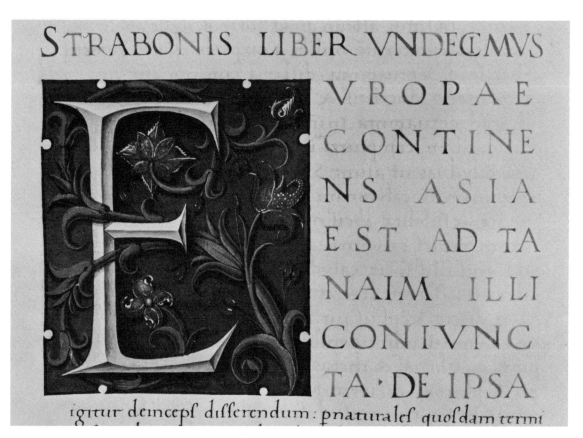

Initial, Strabo, Mantegna and workshop; "Die Situ Orbis," 1459, Bibliotheque Rochegude, Albi.

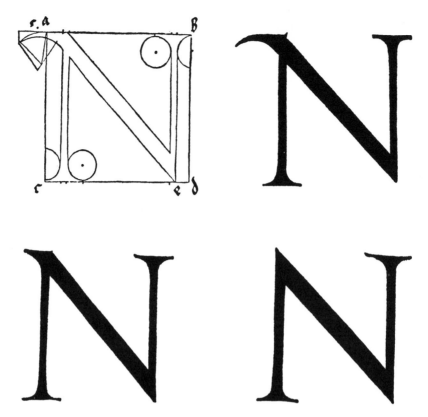

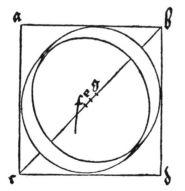

As. o. mach in sein sierung also/reyß in seiner sierung ein Diameter.c.b. vnd teyl den mit ei-
nem puncten.e.in der mitt von einander/vnd setz des pustaben preiten zugs grössen mit zwey
en puncten.f.g. mitten auf den Diameter zů beden seyten neben das.i. die laß zwen centrum
sein/vnd reyß auß yetlichem ein cirkellini die zwo seyten der sierung anrüren/vñ wo dann die zwo cirkellini durcheinander lauffen/da hin zeuch von der hand die dünner preyten des pustaben zug in rech-
ter form. Wie das hernach ist aufgerissen.

As. p. mach in seyn sierung/also/teyl die sierung.a.b.c.d. mit einer zwerchlini.e.f. in der mitt
von einander. Darnach teyl.a.b. vnd.e.f. mit einer zwerchlini.g. h. auch in der mitt von einander. Darnach zeuch den ersten aufrechten preyten zug/des.p. gleych messig wie foren dz·k·

Letter forms by Albrecht Dürer, Nürnberg, 1525.

(Above) Detail of Dubonnet Wall, Paris. Painted letters offer color and contrasts of scale.

(Below) Detail of sign by John H. Hume, Kelso, England. Standard Egyptian letters painted on irregular surface of rough tooled local stone.

(Top) Sign painted on stucco, Nördlingen, Germany.

(Below) Sign painted on cafe window, Amsterdam, Holland.

Gilded wood letter made in United States. Note
similarity to more elegantly proportioned letter shown
on page 78.

(Left) Detail of Container Corporation sign. Metal outlined letters, with body of expanded metal, are projected from brick wall.

(Below) CBS Television symbol, William Golden, Designer.

CBS
TELEVISION
STUDIO

Symbol for New Haven & Hartford Railroad, Herbert
Matter, Designer, 1955.

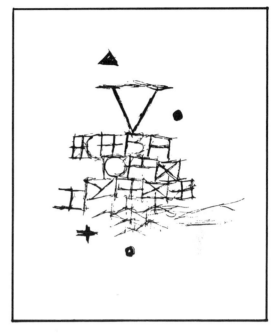

(Above) Untitled pen drawing. Paul Klee, 1918.
Collection: Mr. and Mrs. Arthur A. Cohen, New York.

(Below) Name and number, house in Italy.

Wall of letters, executed in Plexiglas. Composed by
Alvin Lustig for Museum of Modern Art exhibition
"Signs in the Street," 1956. b–Futura, E–Gothic,
a–variation of Clarendon Extended, S–Severain.

Variations on the Egyptian A from "Art Aujourd'hui," 1952.

# ABCD EFGH
# IJKLMNOPR
# QSTUWXYZ

Roman capitals used on Trajan's column, Rome, A.D. 114.

(Above, facing page) Variations of Roman lettering.

(Below, facing page) Perpetua Roman, a classical Roman face. Eric Gill, Designer.

ABCDEFGH
IJKLMNOP
QRSTUVW
XYZ123456
789abcdefg
hijklmnopqr
sſtuvwxyzßſtɛ

ABCDEFGHI
JKLMNOPQR
STUVWXYZ
abcdefghijklmn
opqrstuvwxyz
1234567789&

(Top) Profil, designed by Eugen and Max Lenz, 1946. Three-dimensional capitals and figures; heavy black letters are rimmed with a white line.

(Below) Rockwell, Italic Bold. A bold, full-faced square serif face. Condensed version also designed.

**1 2 3 4 5**

**A B C D E F**

**A B C D E F G H I**
**J K L M N O P Q R**
**S T U V W X Y Z &**
**a b c d e f g h i j k l m n**
**o p q r s t u v w x y z**
**1 2 3 4 5 6 7 8 9 0**

Clarendon, a mid-nineteenth century face.

# ABCDEFGHI
# JKLMNOPQ
# abcdefghijklm
# noprstuwxyz

# 1234567890

abcdef
hiklm
norst
uvwx
z-'.:!?&
gjpqy;
67890
12345,

# A B C D
# E F G H
# I J K L Z
# M N O P
# Q R T U
# S V W X

Heavy sculptured version of Clarendon Extended.
Believed to have been cast in the United States.

# ABCD

---

# EFGHIJKLM
# NOPQRSTUV
# WXYZ12345
# 67890abcde
# fghijklmnopq
# rsſßſttuvwxyz

(Above) A sans-serif face related to Futura Extra Bold with minor variations. The Q has a straight tail starting outside the bowl; the M is splayed and square; the a is similar to Renner Futura, shown below.

Qualitätsarbeit ist gute solide Arbeit

Lehrgänge für fremde Sprachen

Hochschulstadt Mannheim

RUNDFUNKSENDER

# A B C D E F G H I J K L M N O P Q R S T U V W X Y Z

### a b c d e f g h i j k l m n o p q r s t u v

# abcdefghijklmnopqrstuwxyz
# ABCDEFGHIJKLMNOPQR
# STUVWXYZ& 1234567890

(Above) Gill Sans Medium, designed by Eric Gill, 1928.

(Below) Französische Grotesk.

Type face designed by Josef Albers, 1930. An alphabet of capitals and lower case letters, 10 numerals and 10 punctuation marks; accents and special combinations which exist in German are eliminated. Three basic forms are used—the circle, a sector, and a square—which provide symmetrical geometric surfaces; also equal height and width. This font was designed to provide a face with the greatest economy of form for display use.

. il al al

Kombinationsſdhriſt der Metallglas-
Aktiengeſellſdhaft Offenburg Baden

a b c d e f g h i j k l m n o p
q r ſ s t u v w x y z d k 1 2 3
ABCDEFGHIJKLMNO
PQRSTUVWXYZäçš

MODERNISME

*Préciosité*

ÉLÉGANCE

**FORCE**

MONUMENTALITÉ

**SIMPLICITÉ**

**FANTAISIE**

𝕬𝕣𝕔𝕙𝕒𝕚𝕤𝕞𝕖

SÉRIEUX

Physical expression of words–an illustration for
"Construction of the Letter" by Pierre Faucheux,
"Art Aujourd'hui," 1952.

Revised Clarendon letters designed by Elaine Lustig
for Mitten Letters, plaster, 1957.

Detail of entrance sign to Swiss Pavilion, Paris Exposition, 1947. Punched metal letters whose rough edges are in character with scale and shape of letter.

A B C D
E F G H
I K L I
M N

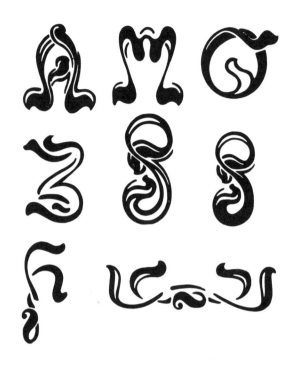

(Facing page, above left) Letters designed by Otto Eckmann, Germany, 1896.

(Facing page, above right) Letters designed by H. van de Velde, from "Van Nu en Straks," Belgium, 1896.

(Facing page, below left) Numerals for Hotel Solvay, Brussels, Belgium, 1895. Victor Horta, Architect.

(Facing page, below right) Advertisement from "Dekorative Kunst," 1898. Designed by Georges Lemmen.

(Below) Shop front, Palma de Mallorca, Spain, c. 1900. Decorative lines of Art Nouveau letters conforms to architecture of building.

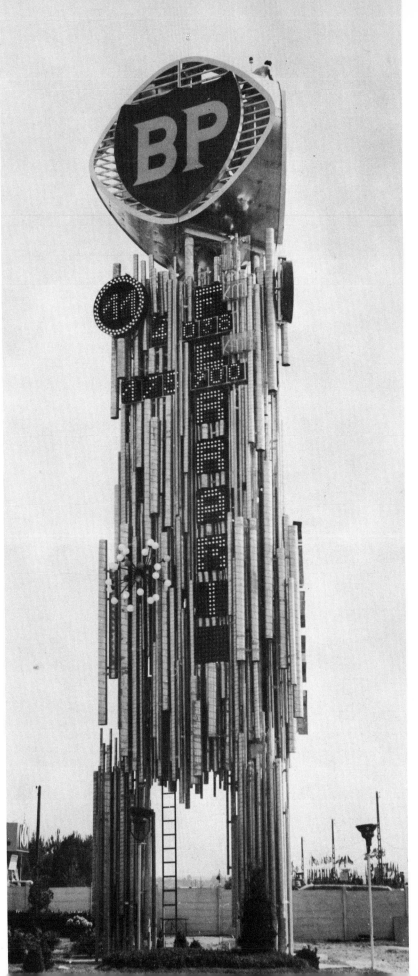

BP Tower, near Le Mans, France, 1960. Jean C
and Andre Poulain, Architects; Michel Charpe
sculptor; Maurice Gasquet, painter. Built by
Société Français de Petroles BP for the Autom
Club of the West to publish race results. Tow
made of steel tubes and electric cables. The s
might have been more pleasantly adapted to the
of the tower, but the structure becomes a h
decorative note in the landscape.

The signpost is an inanimate information bureau. It is often bedecked with devices, symbols, and words by which people are to be guided and informed. It appears throughout history in diverse and complex forms—a sign heralding the approach to an African village; totem poles in North American Indian settlements set up before the houses of different tribes; the watchtower; the beacon; banners; flags; even ceremonial staffs and weapons with heraldic symbols all are emblematic methods of information-giving and attention-getting.

In our contemporary cityscape and landscape, the anatomy of the signpost as well as its objective is equally varied. We can see the anachronistic use of the single lamppost, whose original purpose was to provide a source of light (see page 8), or a steel tube tower—a sculptured poster in metal, specifically designed as an information and advertising tower (see facing page).

The signpost has many purposes, whether isolated in a rural setting, composed within the framework of an industrial campus or shopping center, juxtaposed to a single building to announce its identity, or part of the furniture of the street. Only recently has it become the concern of the planner, the architect and the designer. Too often it is generally seen as an undesigned, undistinguished armature, haphazardly placed in its environs, its symbols and messages inadequately organized and visualized.

In the city the public signpost is seen in an architectural setting. To provide for proper nighttime as well as daytime reading, it should be planned as a component of the lighting system of the city. Placed in an impermanent position on a street, a sidewalk, a safety island, the signpost is seen against a changing chaotic background. Its contribution to the street scene depends on the character of its structure, the appropriateness of its setting and the clarity of its message. Transferred to rural areas, its skeletal structure becomes of primary importance. In relating the signpost to the open landscape (the Olivetti sign, page 117), to a single building (the Mondowmin Tower, page 126) or in competition with billboards, new ideas of space, movement, scale and construction have been employed with inspiring success. It will be interesting to observe how these new signposts will affect the dull rectangular form of the billboard which must undergo a change.

Outdoor advertising companies are making tests on signs which boast such experiments as (1) motion adaptations—pouring, flowing, sparkling, with equal impact day or night; (2) illusion of flowing neon light, writing words and drawing pictures—moving billboard bulletins. The first use of the moving electrical billboard bulletin was on the "New York Times" Building, introduced in June, 1928, to report on the Hoover-Smith elections. It was also effectively used in 1938 at the Paris Exposition. The outdoor advertising companies hope to discourage the use of the standard rectangular bulletin silhouette;

**5 SIGNPOSTS**

they favor completely frameless giant 3-dimensional cutout spectaculars, and plan to introduce weatherproof cardboard popouts which are relatively less expensive compared to glass and plastic displays. Rear screen projection for outdoor posters is also forecast. William Miller, art director of the General Outdoor Advertising Company hopes that "Tomorrow's outdoor advertising will bring more and more of Times Square to hometown main streets."[15]

However, whether in the urban or rural scene, maximum effectiveness at night may result in absence of daytime appeal. Sensible use of materials, logical arrangements of devices and symbols, together with imagination and craftsmanship can produce excellent results in overcoming this difficulty. One need only examine the superb Guimard Entrance Gate of the Paris Subway Station designed at the turn of the century (see page 40), and the excellent London Transport stanchion designed in the fifties for evidence. The Metro stanchion combines a lighting fixture and identification panel; it is completely harmonious as a total design. The London Transport signpost incorporates a light, a time-table holder, a litter bin. Other stanchions, fixed and movable, related to the Underground and Transport series, retain a family likeness, and in spite of the necessity for standardization, there is variety in the materials used, with due concern for appropriateness to locales of different character.

In the organization of expositions and fairs, planners, architects and designers are concerned with moving vehicular as well as pedestrian traffic, with creating open spaces as well as consciously planned cul-de-sacs, and with informing and directing the public. Although expositions are smaller in scale than cities, in these aspects the problems of both are similar. Expositions have been most effective demonstrations of the possible range of architecture and graphic imagery. Heraldry can be incorporated in basic structure and decoration at the same time as in the UK Building (see page 139). Or it can evoke the sculptural solidity of a Gabo or Pevsner, as in the BP tower at Le Mans (see page 104). Here information and publicity are united to create a work of art in a useful object.

Basically the effectiveness of a signpost depends first upon its structure. It can exist as an independent structure–a pylon, a stanchion, a tower, an antenna, a guard post, a screen, a tripod, a pyramid, a jungle gym construction, an entire building (see Futurist Building, page 139), and, at its most extreme, a balloon, anchored but moving, yet fulfilling the demands of a signpost in its relationship to a building (see page 126).

In defining structure of all kinds, Max Bill in "Man and Space" sets down the following principles: "Elementary methods of construction, primary forms, simple numbers, equal elements, lines of the same length." These rules are somewhat akin to many fixed formulae, i.e., the Sivina Proportione of Pacioli, in which Leonardo da Vinci was influential,[17] and the publication of Dürer. The harmonious proportions of architecture, of structure, of letters are based on mathematical truths. These principles are indeed rational, but our creative artists must reinterpret these ideas in their search for new forms as they relate to our growing visual vocabulary.

Display of totem poles, St. Louis Exposition, 1904.

(Above left) Queue shelter and bus stop stanchion, time-table display and litter bins.

(Above right) Holborn Station. Note three-dimensional signs and window sign retain family identity.

(Below) Standard aluminum, queue shelter and London Underground bus stanchion. Queue shelter is fitted with panel for map or poster display. Stanchion carries familiar bus stop sign and related information.

(Facing page, left) Detail of London Underground bus stop stanchion, utilizing the "bulls-eye" design by Edward Johnston and Frank Pick and the sans-serif Edward Johnston letters.

(Facing page, above right) Combined shelter and mast sign, London Underground, Enfield West Station. Adams, Holden and Pearson, Designers.

(Facing page, below right) Typical stairwell entrance to a London Transport Station.

Detail of entrance gate to Metropolitain, Paris subway station. Hector Guimard, Designer, c. 1900. Cast iron frame, amber glass fixtures, painted letters. (See page 40.)

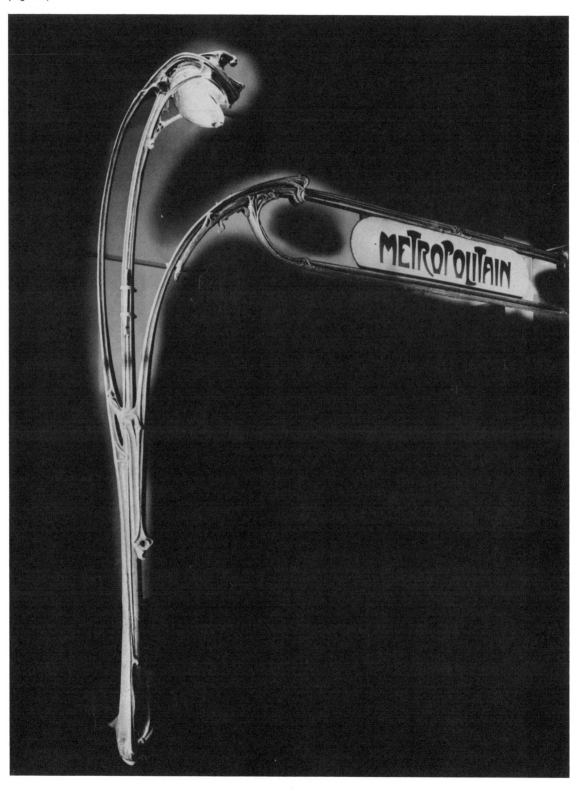

(Top) Swiss signpost, concrete with white letters on a blue ground. Body of arrow is basic shape of sign. Signal SA, Bienne, manufacturer.

(Below right) "Gowshall" illuminated guardpost, 1947. Steel aluminum and glass can be fitted with internal gas or electric light. Gowshall Ltd., Designers. Note illumination on striped poles.

(Below left) Directional post.

(Left) Buller Quay, England, 1856. Monumental letters on a monumental slab incorporated into wall.

(Below) To Stow, Burford and Northleach, England. Symbol and lettering on framed panel affixed to local stone slab.

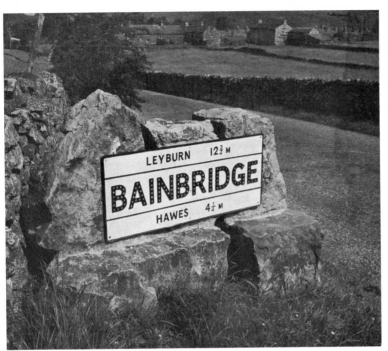

(Top) Bainbridge signpost, England. Practical use of countryside stone. Reflectors on letters enhance illumination; strong letters increase legibility; white background works against stone.

(Center) Frankfurt-Cologne Autobahn. Basic shape is similar; arrowhead more effectively used in Swiss sign shown on page 110.

(Below) Turnpike post and sign. Sign is large, direct, visible; light stanchion behind provides illumination.

(Above) Signpost in France. Note difference in shape of arrow, arrow heads; large condensed capital letters and small standard capitals.

(Below) Signpost in Berne, Switzerland. Light enclosed box employs basic form of the arrow. Heads of arrow differentiated from body. Swiss type face is clear and legible.

(Facing page, left) Antiquated light stanchion and melange of signs, London.

(Facing page, above right) Street sign in colonial Williamsburg, Virginia. An attempt to create a colonial atmosphere.

(Facing page, below right) Street plate in Birmingham, England. Robust lettering from the Victorian era well placed on plate.

(Top) International Landscape Exhibition, Hamburg, Germany. Prof. Hassenpflug, Architect. Leaf symbol used for all advertising, on walls, temporary structures. (See pages 118, 129.)

(Below) Parade Square, Zurich, Switzerland, 1948. Note streetcar lettering, directional signs to Luzern. Consistency and clarity mark the Swiss street signs.

(Above) Advertisement for Olivetti calculator, railroad station, Milan, Italy.

(Below) Billboard along an Italian highway advertising Olivetti teletype machine, 1951. Giovanni Pintori, Designer. Abstract construction in which the linear composition contrasts with sculptural solidity of sheet metal ribbons woven around armature of tubular steel.

(Facing page) International Landscape Exhibition, Hamburg, Germany. Prof. Hassenpflug, Architect. (See page 129.)

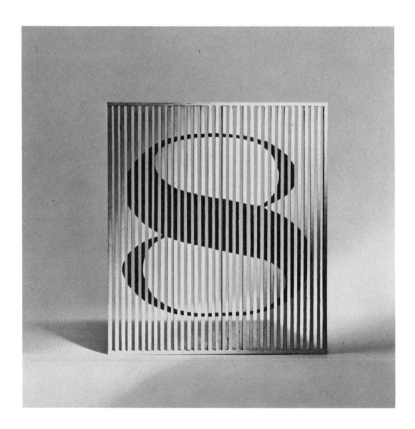

Number for parking lots; International Flight Mall; Roosevelt Field, Inc., Long Island, New York. Webb & Knapp; I. M. Pei Associates, Architects.

Northland Center, Detroit. 1954, Victor Gruen Associates, Architects, Alvin Lustig, Graphics Consultant. (See bottom photograph, page 123.)

Transportation Center, Philadelphia. Vincent G. Kling, Architect.

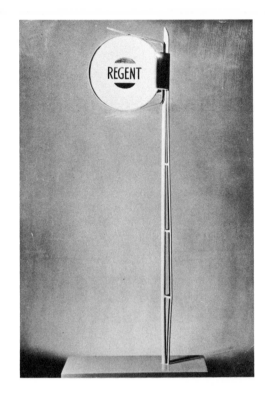

(Above) Garage identification sign, 1954. Regent Oil Co., Ltd., manufacturer; John Barnes, M.S.I.A. of Allen-Bowden, Ltd., Designer. Made of tee iron, sheet aluminum and mild steel. Signal red, aircraft blue, light admiralty gray and white.

(Below) Parking lot stanchions and identification, Northland Center, Detroit.

(Top) Pick up area, Roosevelt Field, Inc., Long Island, New York. Webb & Knapp. I. M. Pei Associates, Architects. Vertical lettering on post emphasized by changes in color. Usually a sans-serif letter provides more continuity.

(Below) Fountain court, parking lot directory. Plexiglas, illuminated from within. Northland Center, Detroit, Michigan. Victor Gruen, Architect.

Northland Center, Detroit. Northland symbol and letter used on water tower; parking lot letters uniform throughout shopping center. (See page 120.)

(Above) Sign suspended from balloon, Tokyo.

(Left) Tower of Mondawmin Shopping Center, Baltimore, Maryland. Elaine Lustig, Designer.

(Top) S. C. Johnson & Son, Administration Building, Racine, Wisconsin, 1938. Frank Lloyd Wright, Architect. Bold letter on water tower contrasts with flow and elegance of structure.

(Below) Waialae Shopping Center, Honolulu, T.M. Victor Gruen, Architect. Stone base, open framework of stanchion make handsome contrast. Verticality of letters echo vertical posts.

Towson Shopping Center, Towson, Maryland, 1959.
Brownjohn, Chermayeff & Geismar, Designers. Tower
is 40 feet high, a steel frame with colored porcelain
enamel panels, recessed lighting.

Trolley information stanchion; single large open metal mesh framed in metal sheet; double tripod stanchion. International Landscape Exhibition, Hamburg, Germany, 1953. Prof. Hassenpflug, Architect.

Tripod stanchion for posters, Hamburg, Germany. Prof. Hassenpflug, Architect.

Totem pole for posters advertising International Landscape Exhibition, Hamburg, Germany, 1953. Note effectiveness of structure contrasted with kiosk.

Advertising towers (left), Pirelli advertising stanchion
(right), Fair in Milan, Italy, 1950.

Pirelli advertising stanchion at Automobile Exhibition, Turin, Italy, 1953. Ed Callahan and Michael Engelmann, Designers.

(Facing page) Exposition Directory in Munich. Richard Roth, Designer. Composed in windmill fashion with colored signposts.

Antenna "Motta," advertising tower at Fair in Milan, 1950.

Telephone booths, Denmark (left), Holland (right),
and Ireland (facing page). Note seventh century uncial
letters are still in use in the 1960's.

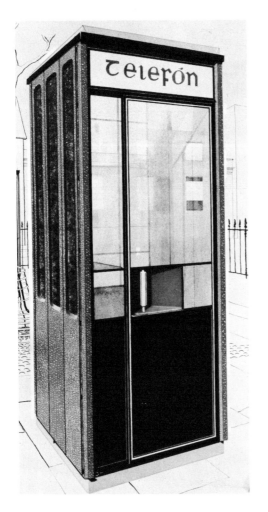

Public ash trays, New York City.

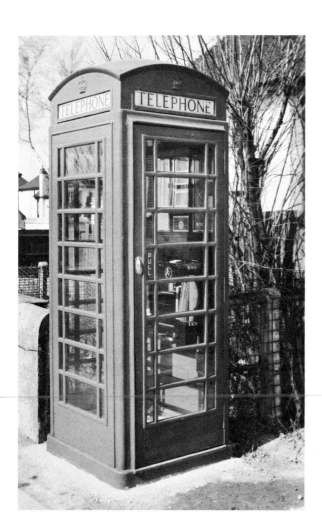

Pavilion of the Book, typographic architecture, for the Casa Editrici Bestetti e Tumminelli e Fratelli Treves, 1927. Fortunato Depero, Architect. At the Third International Biennale at Manza, Italy.

United Kingdom Pavilion, Cape Town, South Africa,
1952. Sir Hugh Casson and Neville Conder, Architects; Sir Hugh Casson, Designer.

"Signs are pre-language, language, and post-language symbols." Man's first symbols stemmed from two sources: his own body–footprints, and his first tools–the arrowhead. In addition, necessity made him produce a third–straight sticks and twigs which could be manipulated to indicate directions.

How these symbols have grown and changed is a subject which cannot be discussed in detail here. However, most of the symbols and pictures we use stem back to these three sources. Man remembers best those symbols which are part of himself, for example the eye, the hand, the pointing finger (pp. 148-149).

When a symbol is sufficiently abstract like the cross, the swastika, the yan and yin, its meaning can be learned, carried down from generation to generation, and its validity as an abstract symbol survives no matter how society changes. On the other hand, symbols that are manufactured–that is to say, symbols or pictures that are the result of changing aspects of industrialization–reach a point of obsolescence. For example, note the symbol for the Sukerhus (page 163). The symbol of the cone of sugar was easily recognizable and communicable for the European society to which it was addressed some thirty or forty years ago. Manufactured sugar has, however, changed its form. Although the symbol is excellent in design and handsomely related in its linear form to the block lettering in the name, it has become archaic as a symbol.

Pointers such as arrows and fingers have more impact than any signs using words.[18] Arrows can be long and thin, short and fat, twisted or straight. They can be solid and open, with tails and without tails. They can be painted on the walls or hung free in the air. Although we have long given up footprints as a directional symbol, the arrow on the street or the road for direction is still in use (see page 153). The arrow consists of shaft, point, and feathering. Klee has said, "The father of the arrow is the thought: how do I expand my reach? Over this river? this lake? that mountain? Symbolically the arrow is direction with point."[19] It can be wood or metal; ornate or plain. It can indicate force, energy and direction; its meaning conveyed by the visual emphasis which the designer imparts to it.

The symbol in feudal days also indicated the professional status of a man. A boot served the cobbler; a mortar and pestle, the druggist; a sheaf of wheat, the baker; a bottle, the tavern owner. But today the descriptive symbol is perhaps the most difficult to design. For example, as Rudolf Modley has indicated, "A little steam engine on a road sign used to warn us of an approaching railroad crossing. It is still supposed to do so in many countries, although it begins to look more like an historic marker. It has little resemblance to the streamlined diesel."[20]

Modley continues, "Arbitrary symbols, such as a plus sign, the question mark, the dollar sign, and the sound symbols of the alphabet are not as easy to learn as the symbols with object 'fidelity.' Yet once accepted, they suffer less from obsolescence. They become tools of our permanent system of visual communication."

Today, more than ever, our symbols must have broad associative meanings, and impart information as well, to serve the complexities of our knowledge and needs. Botanical, chemical, mathematical, medical, monetary, typographical symbols are in universal use–but are not universally understood. Since no verbal alphabet can provide the universal symbol, it remains the task of the designer to communicate a message and to capture the eye. Perhaps he will find the universal symbol for NO PARKING HERE ON SUNDAYS! ! !

# 6 SYMBOLS AND PICTURES

Weathervane, American, c. 1800. A metal staff;
arrow and ball carved of long-leaf, yellow pine.

Weathervane, American, c. 1860. Molded copper and gold leaf; flat letters, three-dimensional horse. Made for breeding farm or racing stable.

Church weathervane, probably Pennsylvania, c. 1850.
Combining musical lyre, tulip form and arrow. Copper
and gold leaf; arrowhead is three-dimensional.

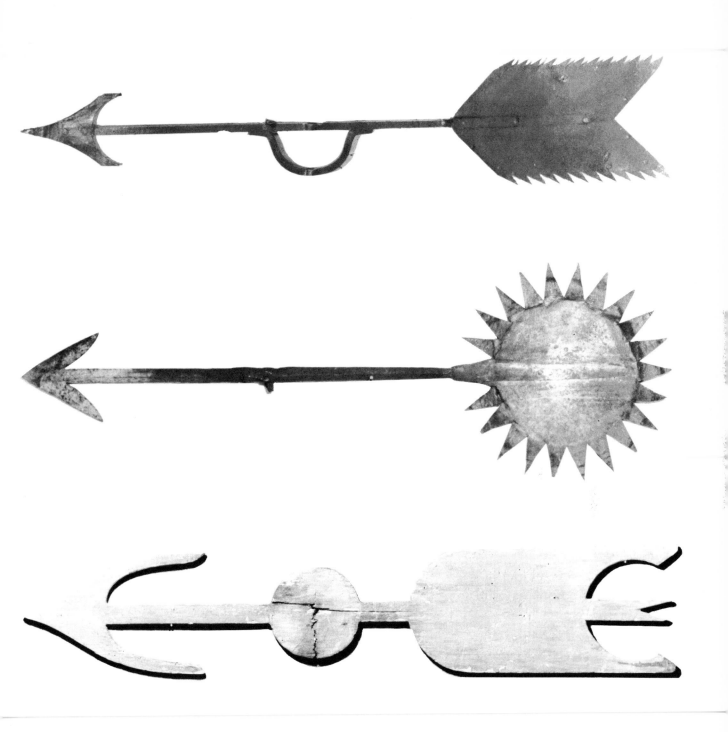

(Above) Sheet iron weathervane, American, c. 1850. (Center) Sunburst church weathervane, American, c. 1800. Made of double sheets of heavy sheet iron, handwrought. (Below) Barn-red painted wood weathervane, Ipswich, Massachusetts. Collection: Mrs. Adele Earnest, Stony Point, New York.

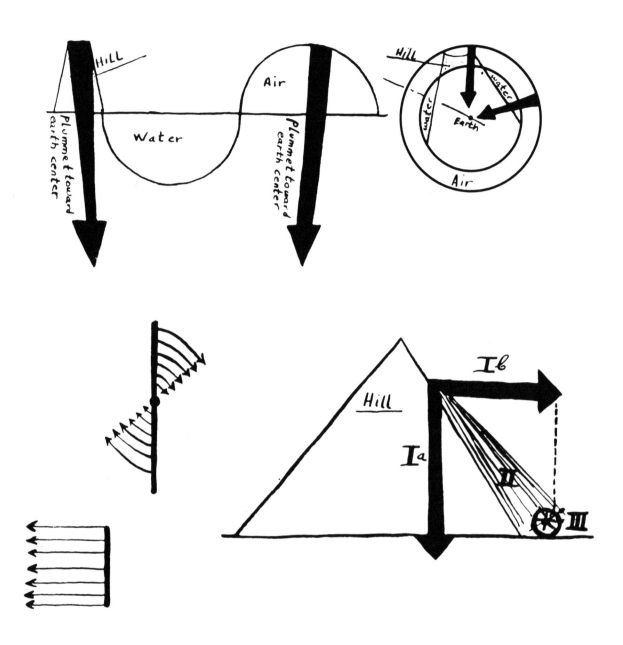

Arrows by Paul Klee, from the "Pedagogical Sketch-book," 1925, edited by Walter Gropius and L. Moholy-Nagy. In the introduction to the 1953 edition, Sibyl Moholy-Nagy writes "true to his inductive creed, Paul Klee demonstrates inner essence and form-giving cause on the most insignificant objects, the spinning top that defies gravity by the centrifugal energy of its gyrations, or the feathered arrow whose path is hampered by gravitational friction . . . Thought and intention that send the arrow on its way are identified with the supra-mechanical force of the Eidos."

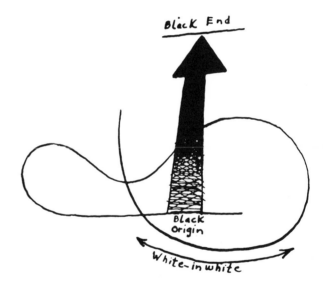

Black End

Black Origin

White-in white

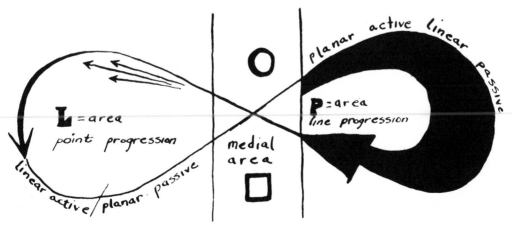

planar active linear passive

○

**P**=area
line progression

**L**=area
point progression

medial
area

□

linear active/planar passive

147

Monument for Vaillant Courturier, 1938. Le Corbusier,
Architect. One of a series of projects by the architect
using the hand as a symbol of gathering, of giving,
of taking. Among other projects is the open hand of
Chandigarh, Pakistan. Le Corbusier has even planned
the hand as an accessible monument.

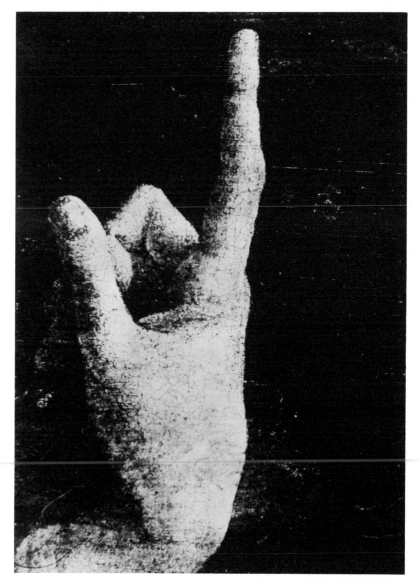

(Above) "The False Mirror." Oil on canvas. René Magritte, 1928. Collection: Museum of Modern Art, New York City. This painting has inspired many commercial symbols, among which is the CBS Television eye. (See pages 84, 162.)

(Below) Detail from "St. John the Baptist" by Leonardo Da Vinci. Collection: The Louvre.

Symbol for Tenth Triennale, Milan, Italy, 1954; designed by Bruno Munari. Stencilled on roads directing traffic to exposition grounds.

(Top left) Arrows emphasizing South, painted on the street, and a stripe echoing the curve of the curb and road.

(Top right) A floor route, painted on the street, with vigorous lettering, lines, and arrows. Chicago.

(Below) Highway, State of Minnesota. Arrow, white line, and metal strips on wood posts all contribute to delineate flow of road.

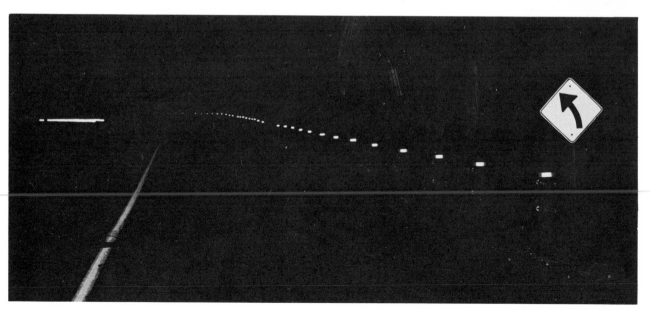

(Top right) Trademark for Goldpfeil, a leather firm. Brass ring and arrow on a natural stone background. Pfeil in German means arrow.

(Below) "Highway." Oil. George Tooker. Collection: Joseph Vernon Reed, New York. The cityscape turns into a nightmare of symbols, lights, faceless authority.

(Above) Movable platform with arrows directing traffic control, England.

(Below) Arrow painted on street surface in Exeter, England.

(Above) Bundle of wheat, a baker's sign, New England, c. 1800. Hand-carved wood, polychromed yellow ochre.

(Below) Sea horse weathervane from the coastal regions of Maine, c. late 1800's. Cut out of 1-inch thick wood board. Collection: Mrs. Edith Halpert, New York.

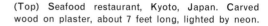

(Top) Seafood restaurant, Kyoto, Japan. Carved wood on plaster, about 7 feet long, lighted by neon.

(Center) Butcher's sign, Pennsylvania, c. 1850's. Carved from hard piece of wood; 18 inches long; a wrought-iron tail, corn cob in mouth.

(Below) Codfish weathervane, Henniker, New Hampshire, c. 1850's. Carved from wood plank, painted green and black. Eye is an ancient shoe button. Collection: Mrs. Adele Earnest, Stony Point, N. Y.

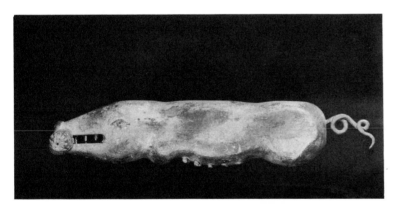

(Directly below; above, facing page) Two views,
Brussel's World's Fair, 1958. Brownjohn, Chermayeff
& Geismar, Designers. Arrows and letters used as
decorative elements.

(Below left) Directional symbol in red on a white ground, to indicate curve on road near Zug, Switzerland.

(Below right) Railroad crossing, the Rimini-Bologna-Piacenza route, 1957.

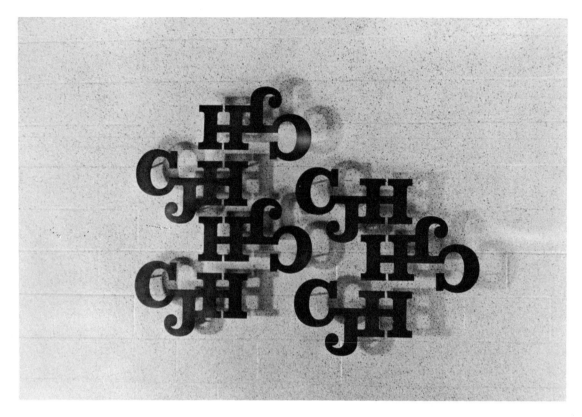

(Facing page, above) Sign for Central Junior High School, Greenwich, Connecticut. Brownjohn, Chermayeff & Geismar, Designers. Brass letters, each 8 inches high, floating off concrete block wall in lobby entrance hall. (Below) CJH symbol, 8 feet high, held by pins away from cement block wall; letters painted blue.

(Above) Sign and symbol for Bertsch & Cooper, Chicago.

(Below) Sign and symbol for Health Organization, Aspen, Colorado. Herbert Bayer, Designer.

(Top left) Symbol for Energol, motor oil, Italy.

(Top right) Matsuya department store symbol, Tokyo.

(Below left) Shirokiya department store, Tokyo. Painted sign on store facade; symbol repeated on flags.

(Below right) Swissair symbol, Bangkok, Thailand. A plastic red circle, white letters on crossbar. This symbol is in use throughout the world, in printed material as well as signs.

Roosevelt Field Shopping Center, Nassau County,
Long Island. Symbol designed by George Pappas,
painted on brick wall. (See page 119.)

CBS Television, Television City, Los Angeles, 1952.
William Golden, Designer. (See page 149.)

# SUKKERHUS

(Above) Candy Shop, Copenhagen, Denmark. Condensed Egyptian letters against outline drawing of old sugar symbol.

(Below) Container Corporation of America initials on plant wall. Condensed letters echo vertical supports.

The street corner has become a conflux of many diverse things. Posts, people and public services abound; in addition to stanchions, we are likely to find a profusion of signs, the ubiquitous arrow, a subway entrance, a newsstand, waste receptacle, letter box and fire alarm. People in a hurry are confronted by a blinking robot that determines if, when and where they move. (But when a vehicle happens to be coming around the corner, the green light does not necessarily mean "go.")

In many of our streets we can see an overburdened stanchion, originally designed to carry only a light. One example (illustrated on page 8) on the corner of a busy street in midtown Manhattan carries as many as 10 different letter forms in 21 different letter sizes which are manufactured in 5 different techniques. The total scene is almost impossible to grasp; the individual messages unreadable in their untidyness.

As confusing as these messages are to the pedestrian, they are even more inaccessible and incomprehensible to the motorist. In addition, there are particular signs addressed to the motorist which carry their own special brand of admonition. For example, having become comfortably conditioned to a left turn on the green arrow, he is suddenly faced with a sign which says "No left turn allowed between 7 A.M. and 12 P.M. Sundays and holidays excepted."

This disarray and disorder is the result of an unimagined, hence unplanned for, growth of public services and traffic. The inability to communicate is further complicated by the mingling of signs that are contradictory and incomprehensible in their language as well as their design. The complexities the eye is offered present no standards; clarity, harmony, legibility, taste, are completely sacrificed. On the other hand, these are the ingredients which make evaluation and understanding possible. Along with fundamental change in pedestrian and vehicular traffic patterns, we need a clarification of communication and directional signs. Only a unified and simplified system based on standards can make our signs accessible to the eye and to the mind.

In the United States, the American Association of State Highway Officials classifies all traffic signs into 3 categories: Regulatory (signs which give notice of traffic regulations such as speed limit, stop, keep right); Warning (signs which call attention to hazardous conditions such as curves, soft shoulders, stops ahead); Guide (signs which show route designations, destinations, such as Bristol 15 Miles, By-Pass).

However, in each state there are many varieties. For example, on street signs in Philadelphia, letters are black on white enameled metal; in Chicago, they are black on yellow. In Baltimore, black letters are seen against white glass panels which transmit natural light during the daylight hours and the light of the street lamp at night. Variations exist in plate size, in materials, in lighting.

**7 STOP AND GO**

A message is communicated by the printed legend, by the shape of the sign, and by the color. Some directional and informational signs have begun to be standardized. For example, the yellow stop sign is on the way out—the red stop signal (red background, white letters) has been gaining acceptance among some states. There has been reluctance on the part of some states due to the fading problem, and the degree of reflection (non-reflective red looks either black or near-black at night), but the almost universal acceptance of red as the color to denote danger has gained favor because, as one road commissioner put it, "recognition does not depend merely on shape and message." More and larger signs do not provide the answer. Nor will censorship, or restriction be effective. Restraint through discipline, and the patient and conscious education of the team responsible for the signs might be a better course; the safety engineers, the sign designers, sign manufacturers, planners and architects all must function with unity of purpose.

Progress has been made in many ways: paint on the city streets offers a versatile control system. The shopping centers, in themselves small cities, have offered solutions for the control of and information about pedestrian and vehicular traffic. Even single, large buildings, which must offer complicated information graphically, have based their solutions on a unity of design (see pages 176-177).

"What a delightful thing's a turnpike road," Lord Byron wrote in "Don Juan" in 1824. In 1961 "Life" magazine calls it "Chaos at Crossroads, Ohio," showing a miscellany of route numbers and eight arrows pointing to four roads. Today turnpike roads have turned into highways and superhighways. There are 250,000 advertising billboards alone across 15,000 cities and towns in the United States. The number of additional directional and informational signs cannot be estimated. The practical needs and purposes of these control devices cannot be served, particularly if they must compete against millions of miles of billboards. (See Chapter 5.)

Some of these difficulties were highlighted in an article entitled "Just you try to find the New England Thruway" by Don Ross in the "New York Herald Tribune."[21] He complained that "many delays were due to indecisions at ambiguous road signs," that many signs "served only to mislead the traveler" and were "ambiguous to the point of meaninglessness." He concluded with a recommendation applicable to all highways and turnpikes, "There is nothing wrong that a half dozen (properly labeled) signs in proper spots wouldn't fix."

But legibility on the road is a more complicated problem. For nighttime and daylight use, high speed visibility and readability become matters of illumination as well. Solutions have been sought through electric light directed onto the sign itself, or by the reflected light of headlights. However, the basic character of the letter, and its relationship to the background are essential factors. The size, shape and weight of the letter, the placement of the words in the frames, the shape and scale of the frames, and the placement of the frames in the landscape are also important elements. In addition is the underlying need for the designer's sense of the proper function of our signs.

Road sign, Pennsylvania Turnpike Commission.

(Top) Street markings, Kelso, England. No possibility of misunderstanding direction.

(Below) "B.C." by Johnny Hart. © 1960, N. Y. Herald Tribune.

(Top left) Do not enter, street markings, Chicago.

(Top right) Left turn only, street markings, Chicago.

(Below left) Bus only, street markings, Chicago.

(Below right) Turn left on arrow, Chicago. Street markings more emphatic than verbal sign.

Road sign, Oklahoma Highway Commission. Clarity
and simplicity.

(Facing page, above) Road sign, Pennsylvania Turn-pike Commission.

(Facing page, below) Road sign, Cumberland County, Pennsylvania Turnpike Commission, 1950. No single identity, but uncluttered and legible signs. (See pages 172, 174.)

Traffic signs, Portland, Oregon, 1950. Clearly visible interior-lighted directional signs with white translucent Plexiglas faces.

Road signs, Pennsylvania Turnpike Commission.
Simplicity of posts, clarity of lettering, provision for
illumination.

Road signs, Division of Highways, California. All signs in Standard faces, upper and lower.

Road signs, Pennsylvania Turnpike Commission. Signs in sans-serif capitals.

Numerals used in Transportation Center,
Philadelphia. Vincent G. Kling, Architect.

(Top) Exit sign in Royal Festival Hall, London.

(Below) Exit sign in Transportation Center, Philadelphia. Italic letters in "To" seem out of place here.

Signs for the Seagram Building, New York City.
Elaine Lustig, Designer.

"People make Woolworths!" the Woolworth Company proudly proclaimed in its report published in 1952 on the occasion of its 75th birthday.[22] The report went on to say that the company "enjoys the customers' preference in any given community to walk into the familiar variety store with the red-and-gold sign across the front." (See page 181.) Yet after seventy-seven years, the company began to abandon its label, changing its identity.

The three illustrations on page 180 indicate the heritage of the F. W. Woolworth empire. In the 1880's each of these shops was similarly identified. The shop fascias carried a simple identification: a light letter, generally Roman in character, was used on a dark background as a decorative band. This use of the fascia as background derives from Roman architecture.

In the seventy-seven-year period there had been very little change in the store-front sign other than the elimination of the words "5 and 10 cent store," in line with the company's shift in merchandising policy. Of course, modifications in the shop sizes and fascias made it necessary to expand or condense the letter but these variations did not detract from the beauty, function, or consistency of the sign.

Although the rounded sculptural letter shapes varied in height, width, and thickness of line, each variation made an effective pattern that retained the characteristics of the Roman letter (see page 182). Thus the Woolworth signs retained their consistency and became synonymous with the "5 and 10 cent store," despite variations in materials (gold-leafed aluminum letters were substituted for wood, painted backgrounds were replaced with porcelain enamel for appearance and ease of maintenance). Two factors apparently dictated the need of developing a new sign to meet current requirements: 1) imitation by other variety stores and 2) growing use of illuminated signs and the possible difficulty of illuminating the red and gold sign.

The adage that imitation is a form of flattery brings to mind two questions: Is it sound economic policy to build up a symbol for 77 years and then abandon it to one's imitators and competitors? Since the red-and-gold sign is synonymous with Woolworth, is it not conceivable that the customer in any variety store believes he is in a Woolworths—since he entered a store with the familiar red-and-gold sign?

Granting the validity of a change under certain circumstances, let us look briefly at some of the trial efforts: the reeded red plastic letter placed directly on a brick wall (see page 184); the same letter protruding above the roofline of the shop but seen against a parapet with a confused pattern of glazed brick (see page 185). In both cases the letter form becomes ugly because of an unusually vulgar use of a new material, with nothing unique or decorative to recommend it. Another effort, a metal, square serif letter, massive in its proportions (note the squared-off O) is set on a straight wall, on a curved fascia, and competes with the "chop suey" lettering on the vertical panels (see page 185). The regularity of the sans-serif letter seems tedious on the fluted fascia. Woolworth is to be congratulated on abandoning these attempts. But it is deplorable to think that the sculptural decoration on the facade is to be abandoned, and that the obsolescence factor rears its head at this point as well.

Lighting experts say that the red and gold sign can be illuminated—and anyone who passes one of the old stores with the familiar sign on a bright, sunny day can observe the effect of light on the modeled letters. On the other hand, with a need for uniformity, as in a shopping center where signs and symbols become a visual problem, perhaps other equally effective and esthetic solutions can be found.

# 8 THE WOOLWORTH STORY

Three companies absorbed in creating the Woolworth empire, c. 1880's. Store fascias carried light letter, generally Roman in character, on a dark background, as a decorative band.

Woolworth store in Princeton, New Jersey.

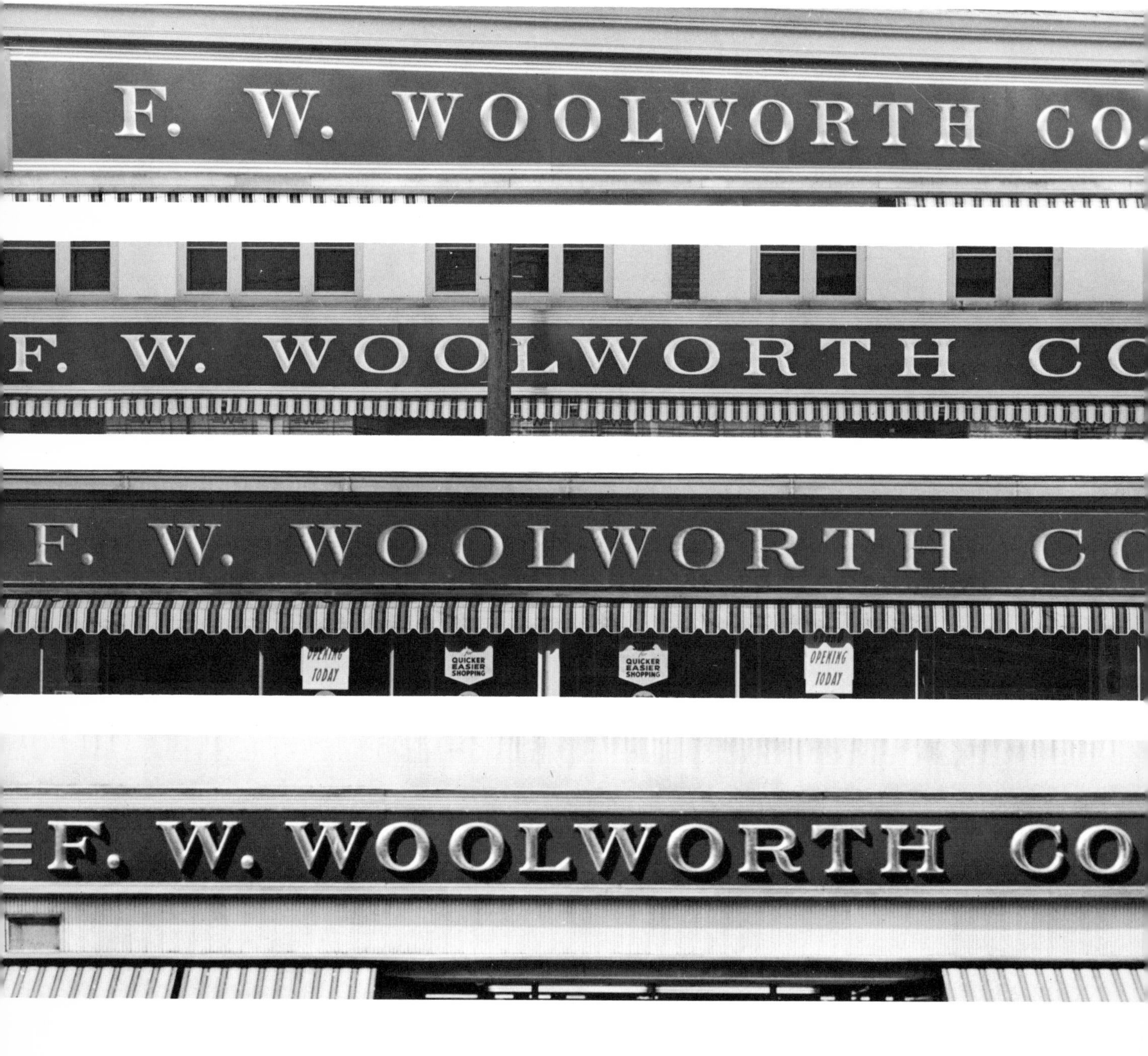
F. W. WOOLWORTH CO.
F. W. WOOLWORTH CO
F. W. WOOLWORTH CO
OPENING TODAY
QUICKER EASIER SHOPPING
QUICKER EASIER SHOPPING
OPENING TODAY
F. W. WOOLWORTH CO

(Facing page) Modifications in store sizes and fascias require expanding or condensing the Roman letter. Note changes in proportion of height to width, variations in stroke from thick to thin. Beauty, function, and consistency not sacrificed.

(Below) Gold-leafed aluminum letters on cement block fascia.

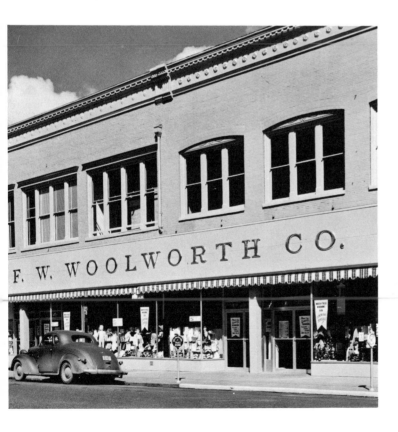

(Top) An unusually vulgar use of
reeded red plastic letter, neither decorative nor legible. (Below) The same letter
form protruding above the canopy line
seen against a parapet containing a confused brick pattern. (Left, facing page)
Three details of letters.

(Top right) Square sans-serif metal letter, massive in proportions, set on straight and curved walls, competes with lettering on vertical panels. San Francisco.

At Yale University, one of the oldest and most progressive educational institutions in the United States, an important and valuable team is at work. An advisory committee to the School of Art and Architecture meets at regular intervals with the staff and students to discuss all phases of work progress and process relative to the subjects taught in this school. Members of the committee include two architects, Gordon Bunshaft of the firm of Skidmore, Owings and Merrill, and Eero Saarinen; two city planners, Catherine Bauer and Edward Bacon; a painter, John Ferren; a sculptor, Theodore Roszak; and a graphic designer, Elaine Lustig. The existence of this advisory committee indicates awareness on the part of some educators and artists of the need for coordination of planning, teaching, and practice in the visual arts. Especially important are those problems made acute by everyday life which must be solved in order to exist in—and enjoy—our twentieth century environment.

For example, the two architects on the committee have always been concerned with the aspects of a building that are related to the other arts. Their concern, particularly in the area of graphics, has been a matter of conscious choice, and their performances can be measured and applauded. Gordon Bunshaft has worked with Herbert Matter and with Ivan Chermayeff (see page 58). Eero Saarinen has worked with Alvin Eisenman, Director of the Graduate Program in Graphic Design at Yale University, and with Elaine Lustig on the General Motors buildings, the American Embassy in London, and the Trans World Airline building at Idlewild. Her notable graphic work for him, as well as for Philip Johnson (see pages 193-197) has helped to impose a harmony on what might have been confusion.

Elaine Lustig designed a display and utility alphabet for use throughout the Seagram Building (see pages 194-195). She feels that two faces are essential in order to help differentiate between the kinds of information stated. For example, Standard Bold Condensed is used for such signs as the fire box, sprinkler connection, light control boxes; and the display alphabet for elevator numbers, rest rooms, and building identification. To indicate the success and range of her cooperation with Philip Johnson, she has worked with him on the Museum of Modern Art and the Brasserie Restaurant in New York City; on the Amon Carter Museum in Fort Worth, Texas; and on the Munson-Williams-Proctor Museum in Utica, New York. In the latter project, it is important to observe how Mrs. Lustig has coordinated the two-dimensional aspects, such as the brochure, and the architectural aspects of a given problem (see page 196).

"Cooperation between designer and architect is possible only if the architect wants help," Mrs. Lustig says. "I feel that the ultimate solution to integration, whether of sculpture, mural painting, graphic arts . . . will result from the creative thinking and organizing ability of but one person—the architect. The graphic designer, if consulted early, can contribute to a whole design. . . . Education should stress general knowledge and appreciation rather than how to do it. At Yale, the students of graphic design are able to carry through certain projects with the architects and city planners. This gives them an opportunity to encounter and familiarize themselves with the problems during the blueprint stages of the work and provides a broad base for application of solutions."[23] Further indication of Mrs. Lustig's interest in the architectural application of graphic design is a plaster three-dimensional letter that she has designed for Mitten Letters, an adaptation of the Clarendon

**9 COORDINATED DESIGN**

Working with the architect I. M. Pei for the past ten years and with a permanent staff of artists, Don Page has met a functional challenge and produced some excellent work. Close contact with the architect in the initial stages of planning has provided Mr. Page with information and inspiration. For example, in the project that I. M. Pei has done for the Ville Marie in Montreal, Mr. Page developed a symbol, based on the building module, for two- and three-dimensional uses, such as the brochure, the window markings (see page 192), and banners. This happy consequence of awareness and similarity of basic aims is not new. Mr. Page points out, "Few architects would give themselves the task of designing the sculpture, or the murals for a building, nor the letters on the buildings. They would, as well, be wise to receive help where graphic problems are involved."

Whether the result of planning on a corporate level or of the vigilance of individual architects, a renaissance is evident in our use of signs. Victor Gruen, architect and planner involved in large commercial and industrial projects as well as single buildings, works with the graphic departments in his own offices, in Detroit or in San Francisco. Sometimes he works with a single graphic consultant, as he did with Alvin Lustig for the shopping center, Northland, in Michigan (see pages 120, 121).

In the "Architectural Record," Mr. Gruen stated, "The importance of graphic design in architecture extends beyond buildings proper. Signs that regulate traffic, signs that direct people toward buildings or other areas, signs that advertise– all of these influence structures and environments and therefore legitimately belong in the field of architectural design. The architect will reach his greatest effectiveness not simply when he heeds the demands of his client concerning signs, but also when he can analyze the owner's true needs and tastefully interpret them–often by means other than signs, as by symbols, colors, shapes, etc. This must, of course, be done to the client's satisfaction and with an effect of elegance and of gaiety or dignity, as occasion requires. When it is generally acknowledged that our architecture must be the total expression of all the facets and forces of our times, when we as architects do not shy away from those things we dislike, but try to improve them–then the way will be open to a better, more complete expression in commercial architecture."[24]

Ivan Chermayeff and Thomas Geismar have worked with Gordon Bunshaft of Skidmore, Owings and Merrill on the Chase Manhattan Bank in New York, on Libby-Owens-Ford in Toledo, Equitable Life, the United Airlines Terminal at Idlewild, and First City National Bank of Houston, Texas. Chermayeff says, "It has become evident that the wording, the placement, and the detailing of lettering are all important aspects of the problem. They must all be thoroughly studied in order to achieve consistent identification throughout a building. Consideration therefore is given not only to major signs, but also to door identification, mail chutes, fire alarm boxes, and all other points that are normally left up to the suppliers. The most satisfying results are achieved when all signs are as readable as suits their function, as consistent with one another as common sense will allow, and as integrated with the architecture as good taste makes possible."[25]

The list of architects and designers devoted to the concept of coordinated design continues to grow. Marcel Breuer, whose office has included graphic designers for more than a decade, has produced outstanding results in the building for Van Leer in Holland; and in the Bijenkorp and Cineac buildings in Rotterdam (see pages 59, 60). Raymond and Rado have consistently engaged the services of such professional experts as Ladislav Sutnar (see page 201).

Coordinated design is possible as an aspect of business. Abbott Laboratories, a conservative company that manufactures and markets pharmaceutical products, has emphasized graphics and the arts in its advertising and institutional programs. It has extended its design program into packaging, labels, and letterheads; George Nelson Associates has been engaged to unify visually all the organs of company contact with its functionaries and the public, to charge this image with clarity, color, and taste and thereby project a company personality which would sharply distinguish it from competing firms in its area. This program includes all company papers, stationery, invoices, contract forms, packaging and labels, exhibits, architecture, interiors, and advertising. One of the first solutions has been the development of a symbol, a geometric A, dramatic and unique, which is used in a variety of ways (see pages 204-205).

An exceptional development is that of the International Business Machines Company which has employed architect and industrial engineer Eliot Noyes as consultant. He has designed new products and several new buildings and has recommended other architects for various plants and buildings. In addition, he has brought in graphic designer Paul Rand for an extensive program involving building and property signs, machine signs, as well as printed material. In the interest of a consistent and recognizable visual identity for the company, the team of Noyes and Rand has come up with a program for standardizing building and property signs for all locations. In order to remedy what Mr. Noyes calls a "babel of messages transmitted, no single message clearly received," he suggested the following questions for consideration:

- In signs using the company name is the Corporation clearly and consistently identified?
- Are signs used intelligently in relation to buildings as elements of architecture?
- Are other company signs being handled consistently as to text (message) and symbols (arrows, etc.)? As to structure, color, type faces?
- Do all signs represent and, in a sense, identify the company through their design?
- Does the sign program appear dignified and acceptable to the outside world, or is it adding to the general visual clutter and confusion?
- Are there economies to be found?

Among Mr. Noyes' observations was the simple recognition that IBM buildings usually have the company name on them. All too rarely has the sign been considered as an element of the architecture—and a prominent element at that. After a good deal of study, and testing, several solutions were reached. Instead of a vertical rectangle for the shape of the sign, a square in four different sizes was employed. They codified the manner in which lettering and arrows are used and engineered structures to support the signs in various materials and finishes to produce a standardized appearance. A type face that Paul Rand had at first recommended was Standard Medium Condensed in upper and lower case letters (see page 199). It was chosen because he felt it enabled the designer to put rather long words in fairly short spaces; and because he believed it would be thoroughly legible to motorists. Further testing for legibility (important at really high speeds) led to a modification; Standard Medium was finally selected (see page 199). Incidentally, it was the type face that led designers Noyes and Rand to the modification in the form of the signs. Mr. Noyes believes that "with a codification, the signs on IBM property all over the world will present a clear, dignified, and unified appearance of quality, consistent with the nature and spirit of the company."[26]

Schools on all levels today are emerging from their static state; no longer are they merely mechanisms for the transferring of information. The re-activation of the intellectual level of our teaching, the intensive and challenging work offered students by faculties in combination with outside consultants points the way to our schools becoming "proving grounds" for ideas. The school is in the process of becoming a place for cooperative and creative relationships between student, educators and men of experience. In this country many programs like the one at Yale University are in operation; projects are being developed at the University of Illinois, in Urbana and at Pratt Institute in New York. In schools abroad–the Royal College of Art in London, the Hochschule für Gestaltung in Ulm, Germany, and the University of Cordoba in Argentina–coordinated education in the visual arts is under way.

View of model of building looking north, Central City
Project, New York City, 1960. Webb & Knapp. I. M.
Pei & Associates, Architects. Note sign and symbol
on roof. Part of the building will be leased to the
General Post Office.

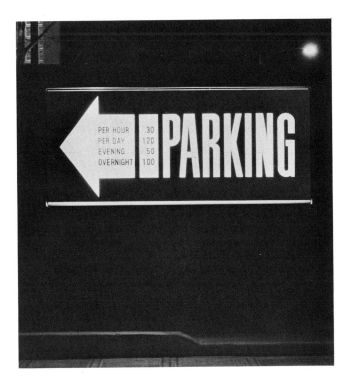

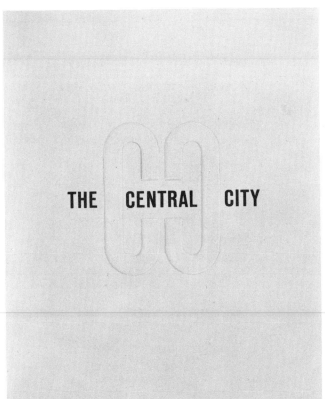

(Above) Parking sign, Denver Hilton Hotel, Denver, Colorado, 1959. I. M. Pei & Associates, Architects; Walter Kacik, Designer. Aluminum, with cut-out letters, backed with plexiglas and lighted from within.

(Below) The Central City logo on brochure.

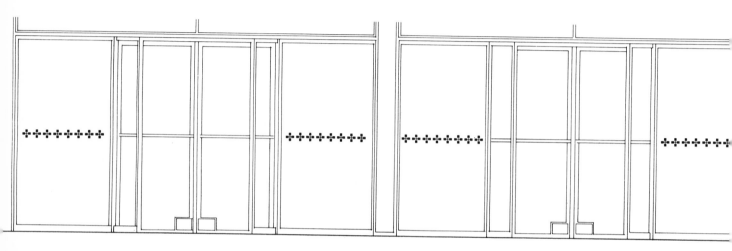

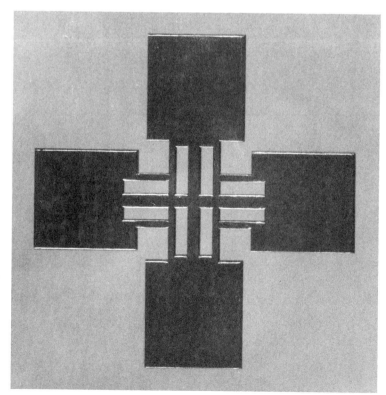

(Above) Drawing of one of the entrances to the office tower of the Place Ville Marie, Montreal, Canada, 1960. I. M. Pei & Associates, Architects and Planners. Symbol, designed by Kenneth Resen, is sandblasted on glass between revolving doors, thus eliminating need for black squares or strips. Red and white flags which will carry the symbol are planned for the plaza.

(Below) Symbol is also used in brochure, designed by the Graphics Department, I. M. Pei & Associates.

(Above) Sign, Brasserie Restaurant, New York City, 1960. Philip Johnson, Architect; Elaine Lustig, Designer. Bronze box with letters cut out of face; fluorescent illuminations from behind; boxes placed on both sides of entrance.

(Below) 375 Park Avenue, Seagram Building, New York City, 1959. Mies van der Rohe and Philip Johnson, Architects; Elaine Lustig, Designer. Bronze numerals on spur travertine wall; placed on both sides of glass enclosed lobby.

# LOWER LOBBY

FIRST FLOOR DIRECTIONS TO PHONES etc., IN CELLAR
SCALE FULL SIZE

NOTE:
LETTERING TO BE 5'-6" FROM FLOOR LINE CENTERED ON RIGHT HAND HALF OF DOORS ONLY

# BASEMENT

# WOMEN

# MEN

FLOORS 2-38 TOILET IDENTIFICATION

NOTE:
LETTERING TO BE 5'-0" FROM FLOOR LINE, CENTERED ON DOOR

# PLAZA

FIRST FLOOR EXIT SIGNS IN STAIRS NUMBERS 3 AND 4
SCALE: FULL SIZE

NOTE:
LETTERING TO BE 5'-0" FROM FLOOR LINE, CENTERED ON DOOR

# 14

FLOORS 2-38 FLOOR IDENTIFICATION
IN STAIRS

NOTE:
LETTERING TO BE 5'-0" FROM FLOOR LINE

# 2 - 10

# 26 - 3

# 11 - 25

ELEVATIONS OF FIXTURE "W"
(BACK LIGHTED LUCITE NUMERALS
SET IN MARBLE PANELS
SCALE: FULL SIZE

# STANDPIPE A

BRONZE LETTERING FOR STANDPIPE AL
SCALE: FULL SIZE

**Worksheet for display and utility alphabets designed by Elaine Lustig for Seagram Building, New York City.**

A B C D E F G

H I J K L M N

O P Q R S T U

-V W X Y Z , " "

2 3 4 5 6 7 8 9

DISPLAY ALPHABET
NO SCALE

A B C D E F G H I J K L

M N O P Q R S T U V W

X Y Z - . , " " 1 2 3 4

5 6 7 8 9 0    &

UTILITY ALPHABET
NO SCALE

(Top) Brochure, Munson-Williams-Proctor Institute, Utica, New York, 1960. Philip Johnson, Architect; Elaine Lustig, Designer. Brochure describing the museum and its activities, published on the occasion of opening of new building. (Below) Name on the facade of the building. Note use of italic letter for brochure and roman face for facade.

**Balcony**

Galleries
Founders' Room
Thomas Cole Room

**Main Floor**

Galleries
Art Shop
Associates' Room

**Ground Floor**

Auditorium
Lending Libraries
Offices
Rest Rooms

**Basement**

Tunnel to School of Art

(Above) View of floor directory and elevator, Munson-Williams-Proctor Institute. Note how textured wall panel has been used as a background for the plexiglas panel. (Below) Close-up of directory. The straight-forward typography, its placement on panel and shape of panel relate both to signal box and to elevator.

(Top) IBM Building, Fifty-seventh Street and Madison Avenue, New York City.

(Below) IBM Building, Rochester, Minnesota. Elliot Noyes, Architect; Paul Rand, Designer. Each building calls for a special solution, but a family identity is retained.

(Above) Sign at IBM plant, Poughkeepsie, New York. White letters are placed on red and blue.

(Below) Sign at IBM plant, Poughkeepsie, New York. Standard medium lettering replaces the condensed font shown above. Note change of format from rectangle to square.

IBM Mohansic Research Laboratory, Mohansic, N. Y.
This shape is expressive of the flag concept—considerable background color beyond that used by letters. Lettering is placed at bottom because sign must be visible as one approaches building up a flight of steps. Note that Condensed Standard is used here.

Addo-X showroom, Mexico City, D. F., 1958. Ladislav Sutnar, Designer. Signs on ceiling, wall and free-standing wall become the architecture of the building.

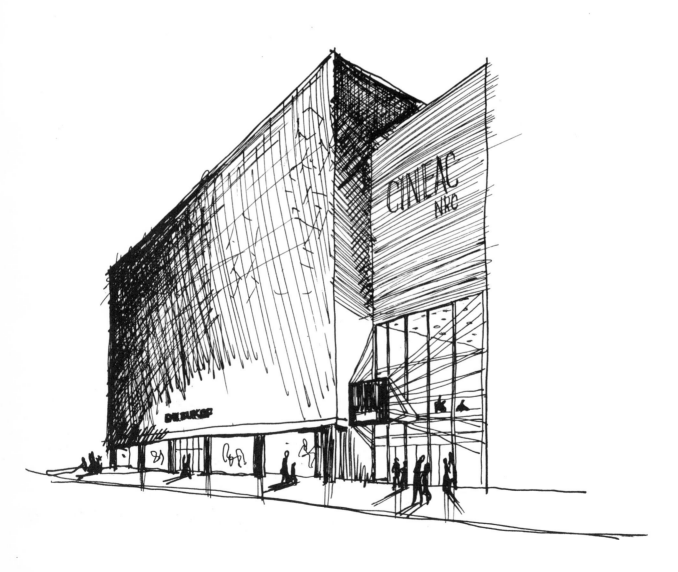

# BIJENKORF

(Facing page) Artist's rendering of de Bijenkorf and Cineac. (See pages 59-60.)

(Above) Lettering for de Bijenkorf department store, Rotterdam, Holland, 1953. Marcel Breuer and A. Elzas, Architects; Daniel Schwarzman, Consultant.

(Below) Van Leer Office Building, Amsterdam, Holland, 1959. Marcel Breuer, Architect. A free-standing, illuminated structure.

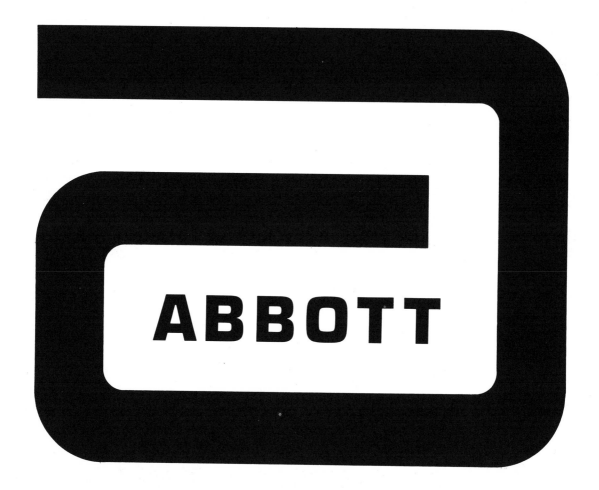

(Facing page) Abbott A. George Nelson Associates, Designer. Symbol used by Abbott Laboratories on stationery, invoices, labels, packages, advertising, exhibits and architecture.

(Below) Abbott Laboratories, Research Building, N. Chicago, 1960. George Nelson Associates, Designer. Name and symbol in stainless steel and plexiglas.

**NOTES**

1. Le Corbusier, WHEN THE CATHEDRALS WERE WHITE, p. 8.

2. ARCHITECTURAL FORUM, August, 1955, p. 123.

3. ARCHITECTURAL REVIEW, June, 1955; October, 1956; December, 1956.

4. ARCHITECTURAL RECORD, January, 1958, John Knox Shear, p. 125.

5. Walter Schwagenscheidt, EIN MENSCH WANDERT DURCH DE STADT, Germany, 1957.

6. At a symposium at the Museum of Modern Art in 1954 the question "Would you change Broadway?" was asked of the speakers. Subsequently this question was asked of Jose Luis Sert and Lewis Mumford by the author. The lines quoted are from conversations with these people.

7. ARCHITECTURAL FORUM, August, 1955.

8. See note 6.

9. ARCHITECTURAL REVIEW, December 23, 1950, p. 384.

10. Le Corbusier, op. cit., "The Fairy Catastrophe," p. 83.

11. Walter Winchell, DAILY MIRROR, September 20, 1956.

12. ARCHITECTURAL REVIEW, June, 1959.

13. Excerpts from a letter written by George Nelson to Mildred Constantine after his first visit to Brasilia in April, 1960.

14. Millard Meiss, ANDREA MANTEGNA AS ILLUMINATOR.

15. "Can New Techniques Expand Sales?" PRINTER'S INK, October 9, 1959.

16. Max Bill, MAN AND SPACE.

17. Fra Luca de Pacioli, DE DIVINA PROPORTIONE, 1509. (Pacioli was a mathematician who worked with Piero della Francesca and Leonardo da Vinci.)

18. Charles Morris, SIGNS, LANGUAGE AND BEHAVIOR.

19. Paul Klee, PEDAGOGICAL SKETCHBOOK.

20. Rudolf Modley in a letter to Mildred Constantine. (See bibliography.)

21. NEW YORK HERALD TRIBUNE, February 27, 1959.

22. WOOLWORTH'S FIRST 75 YEARS, 1879-1954, F. W. Woolworth Co., New York, 1954.

23. ARCHITECTURAL RECORD, September, 1956.

24. Op. cit.

25. Ivan Chermayeff in a letter to Mildred Constantine.

26. ARCHITECTURAL RECORD, June, 1960, p. 157.

Ballinger, Raymond, LETTERING IN MODERN USE, Reinhold Publishing Corp., New York, 1954.

Cassirer, Ernest, LANGUAGE AND MYTH, Harpers, New York, 1946.

Dürer, Albrecht, UNDERWEYSUNG DER MESSUNG, Nürnberg, 1525.

Gray, Nicolete, LETTERING ON BUILDINGS, Architectural Press, London; Reinhold Publishing Corp., New York, 1960.

Hayakawa, S. I., LANGUAGE IN ACTION, Harcourt Brace, New York, 1941.

Kepes, Gyorgy, LANGUAGE OF VISION, Paul Theobald and Company, Chicago, 1947.

–NEW LANDSCAPE, Paul Theobald and Company, Chicago, 1956.

Klee, Paul, BAUHAUSBUCHE II, Edited by Walter Gropius and L. Moholy-Nagy, 1925.

–PEDAGOGICAL SKETCHBOOK, Translated by Sibyl Moholy-Nagy, Frederick A. Praeger, New York, 1953.

Le Corbusier, WHEN THE CATHEDRALS WERE WHITE, Reynal & Hitchcock, New York, 1947.

Meiss, Willard, ANDREA MANTEGNA AS ILLUMINATOR, Columbia University Press, New York, 1957.

Modley, Rudolf, THE CHALLENGE OF SYMBOLOGY, Fund for the Advancement of Education, Ford Foundation, New York, 1959.

Moholy-Nagy, L., VISION IN MOTION, Paul Theobald and Company, Chicago, 1956.

Morris, Charles, SIGNS, LANGUAGE AND BEHAVIOR, George Braziller, New York, 1955.

Nerdinger, Eugen, BUCHSTABENBUCH, Verlag Callwey, Munich, 1954.

Nettelhorst, Leopold, AUSSENVERBUND, Verlag Callwey, Munich, 1952.

Reiner, Imre, MODERN AND HISTORICAL TYPOGRAPHY, Paul A. Struck, New York, 1946.

Tschichold, Jan, DIE NEUE TYPOGRAPHIE, 1928.


ARCHITECTURAL FORUM, August, 1955; August, 1958; September, 1960.

ARCHITECTURAL RECORD, September, 1956, pp. 242-272, "Signs and Symbols"; June, 1960, pp. 149-164, "Architectural Graphics."

ARCHITECTURAL REVIEW, November, 1953, Nicolete Gray, "Theory of Classical Lettering"; June, 1954, Nicolete Gray, "Egyptian Lettering"; June, 1955, "Outrage"; October, 1956, "Counterattack"; December, 1956, "Counterattack"; February, 1958, D. Dewar Mills and Kenneth Browne, "Townscape"; June, 1959, September, 1959, Kenneth Browne, "Townscape."

ART BULLETIN, June, 1960, Millard Meiss, "Toward a More Comprehensive Renaissance Palaeography."

ARTS AND ARCHITECTURE, August, 1960, Gyorgy Kepes, "The Visual Arts Today."

ART AUJOURD'HUI, 1952. (Whole issue)

ARTS IN LOUISVILLE, No. 2, October, 1955, Grady Clay, "Townscape."

BEISPIELE KUNSTLERISCHE SCHRIFT, 1900, 1902, 1906, 1910, 1926. Edited by Rudolf von Larisch; Verlag Anton Schroll, Vienna.

**BIBLIOGRAPHY**

DESIGN, London, September, 1954. (Whole issue)

DEUTSCHE BAUZEITSCHRIFT, January, 1959, Gottfried Prolss, "Die Werbeschrift in der Architectur."

ESTHETIQUE INDUSTRIELLE, No. 39, Paris, 1960. (Whole issue)

HAAS'SCHE SCHRIFTGIESSEREI, A. G., Munich, 1960. (Type specimen book)

JOURNAL OF THE AMERICAN INSTITUTE OF ARCHITECTS, March, 1961, "Urban Design." (Whole issue)

PENROSE ANNUAL, London, 1952, Nicolas Pevsner, "Festival of Britain Lettering."

TYPOGRAPHICA 13, London, 1957. (Whole issue)

WARD & CO., Bristol, England, 1960. (Type specimen book)